ENERGY PRICES, INFLATION, AND ECONOMIC ACTIVITY

ENERGY PRICES, INFLATION, AND ECONOMIC ACTIVITY

Edited by
KNUT ANTON MORK
M.I.T. Energy Laboratory

Center for Energy Policy Research
Massachusetts Institute of Technology

BALLINGER PUBLISHING COMPANY
Cambridge, Massachusetts
A Subsidiary of Harper & Row, Publishers, Inc.

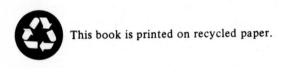
This book is printed on recycled paper.

Portions of this work were prepared under grants from the National Science Foundation and the United States Department of Energy. The United States Government reserves a royalty free, nonexclusive and irrevocable license to reproduce, publish or otherwise use, and to authorize others to use, for United States Government purposes, all copyrighted material resulting from the work performed under said grants.

International Standard Book Number: 0−88410−691−8

Library of Congress Catalog Card Number: 80−21348

Printed in the United States of America

Library of Congress Cataloging in Publication Data

MIT Center for Energy Policy Research Conference on Energy Prices,
  Inflation, and Economic Activity, Cambridge, Mass., 1979.
  Energy prices, inflation, and economic activity.

  Bibliography: p. 157
  Includes index.
  1. Petroleum products—Prices—Mathematical models. 2. Economic
history—1945—Mathematical models. 3. Energy policy—Mathematical
models. 4. Inflation (Finance)—Mathematical models. 5. Unemployment. 6. Business cycles.
I. Mork, Knut. II. MIT Center for Energy Policy Research. III. Title.
HD9560.4.M18 1979   333.79   80−21348
ISBN 0−88410−691−8

CONTENTS

LIST OF FIGURES

LIST OF TABLES

ACKNOWLEDGMENTS

The papers presented here were originally prepared for the M.I.T. Center for Energy Policy Research conference on Energy Prices, Inflation, and Economic Activity in Cambridge, Massachusetts, November 9–11, 1979. The encouragement and financial resources made available by the Center for Energy Policy Research were crucial for the publication of this volume. The task of editing the book has been a laborious, but gratifying, experience. I wish to thank the various authors for their cooperation in the process of revising and editing the papers for publication. I also want to express my gratitude to Peter Heron for his excellent editorial assistance, and last, but not least, to Alice Sanderson and her group for their efficient technical assistance in preparing the manuscript.

Cambridge, June 1980
The Editor

1 ENERGY PRICES, INFLATION, AND ECONOMIC ACTIVITY
Editor's Overview

OPEC's decision to quadruple the price of oil in 1973 shook the economics profession as much as it shook the world. From being confined to a corner of the area of industrial organization, the economics of energy became—almost overnight—one of the most popular subjects of economics. Macroeconomists as well as microeconomists became interested, for it soon became clear that the impact of the 1973–1974 oil price shock would not be restricted to a few isolated markets. On the other hand, the relevance of this experience for policy decisions in the future did not seem obvious. For, as time went on, the world market for oil seemed to stabilize, the economy recovered from the recession, and the events of 1973–1975 seemed to be a one-time experience.

As it turned out, we were not that lucky. In early 1979, at the time of the Iranian revolution, the world price of oil started to rise again and nearly doubled in a few months. Gasoline lines reappeared after five years of absence, and a new round of inflation and economic slowdown seemed to be imminent. Moreover, it was recognized that further surprises might be lying ahead, as the behavior of oil prices in late 1979 indeed confirmed. Like the proverbial poor, energy price shocks seem to be with us—at least for some time to come. And as the problem remains, so will the need for research and improved understanding of the issues.

In recognition of this need, the M.I.T. Center for Energy Policy Research (CEPR) organized a research conference in November 1979, where the results of several research efforts in this area were presented. CEPR had already sponsored one of these efforts for some time—that of Knut Anton Mork and Robert E. Hall. It was felt, however, that the time had come to bring the various researchers in this area together, to compare results and look for consensus. Most of the papers presented at this conference have been revised into the following chapters of the present volume.

Two of the chapters present results based on large short-run macroeconomic models, which have been modified to facilitate the analysis of energy price shocks. The Data Resources, Inc. (DRI) Model, which underlies Otto Eckstein's analysis in Chapter 4, has been developed to represent the energy sector in quite some detail; whereas the MPS model, which is used by Stephan Thurman and Richard Berner in Chapter 5, relies on ad hoc adjustments to a somewhat larger extent. These two models are typical examples of large macroeconomic models that had been used for short-term forecasting and policy analysis long before the oil shock in 1973. The changes and adjustments made in these models are also typical of the increased awareness of the importance of events in energy markets for macroeconomic analysis. Equally typical are the difficulties the model-builders have encountered in the process of modifying the respective models for the analysis of energy price shocks. Because energy price shocks are so different from the previous applications of these models, the adjustments would either have to be ad hoc or require substantial restructuring of these very large models.

A different kind of large model is used by Richard J. Goettle in Chapter 6. Basing his work on the Brookhaven National Laboratory/ Dale Jorgenson Associates (BNL/DJA) energy-economy model system, he studies the long-term effects of alternative energy policies on aggregate supply and economic growth. Abstracting from the shock effects in the short run, this model framework permits a closer focus on the issues of energy substitution, industry structure, and long-run growth potential. Cost–benefit analyses come naturally out of this framework.

Just as the BNL/DJA model system emphasizes the supply side of the economy, the short-run macroeconomic models highlight the forces of aggregate demand. Recognizing the importance of both issues, Knut Anton Mork and Robert E. Hall have set forth to build an integrative framework that incorporates the two approaches. Their effort has resulted in a relatively small model, so their analysis, which is presented in Chapter 3, does not benefit from the great detail of the other models presented in this volume. On the other hand, their analysis may be said to present a more coherent story about the various forces at work in the economy in a period immediately following an energy price shock.

Although this volume presents some of the most important research efforts on the problems of energy price shocks, it does not cover the large body of previous work in this area. Neither do the model-based chapters discuss all the issues involved. A broader discussion of the issues, as well as previous research, is presented in Robert S. Dohner's survey in Chapter 2. Going beyond the sometimes overmechanical discussions that come out of quantitative models, Dohner introduces the reader to the conceptual and cognitive issues that are important elements of an improved understanding of the relationships between energy markets and the macroeconomy.

Dohner emphasizes the conceptual and practical differences between the regular case of imported inflation and increases in the prices of imported inputs to production, such as energy. Whereas imported inflation usually brings real economic expansion as well as inflation, an increase in energy prices results in the unhappy, though familiar, combination of increased inflation and reduced economic activity. Dohner discusses the various aspects of the effects on aggregate demand and aggregate supply and considers in some detail the possible effects of energy price increases on the wage-price inflationary spiral.

Many of these issues are discussed by the other authors as well. Thus, Thurman and Berner emphasize the difference between changes in energy prices and other import price changes and apply the distinction in an analysis of the effects of having world oil prices quoted in units of Special Drawing Rights (SDR) rather than the dollar. The role of aggregate supply is emphasized by Goettle and by Mork and Hall; and Eckstein presents his Core Inflation Model as a special condensed representation of the wage-price spiral in the DRI model.

Mork and Hall, Eckstein, and Thurman and Berner all analyze the macroeconomic effects of the 1979 energy price shock. Because the underlying research was done at slightly different times over a period when conditions changed rapidly, and because other assumptions differ somewhat as well, the results are not directly comparable. Nevertheless, all the models agree that the effects on inflation, real growth, and employment are likely to be substantial. Compared to the other authors, Mork and Hall predict a quicker return to normal employment levels, which reflects their general belief in the ability of the economy to recover quickly from any kind of shock. On the other hand, their analysis suggests a substantial permanent reduction in output and disposable income, because of the adverse effect on aggregate supply. Eckstein differs from the others by predicting a more prolonged effect on inflation. Of the authors represented in this volume, Eckstein appears to be the most pessimistic as to the prospects of lowering inflationary expectations in the short and intermediate run.

The various authors also discuss macroeconomic policies that could mitigate the effects of energy price shocks. They all agree that the choice between policies to offset inflation on the one hand and unemployment on the other is much more painful in this situation than in many other instances, because energy price shocks increase inflation and unemployment at the same time.

They also agree that any attempt to eliminate the energy-induced increase in inflation by conventional macroeconomic policy tools will be very costly in terms of unemployment and loss in real output and income. The prospects for shoring up unemployment seem brighter, but at the cost of higher inflation rates either now or in the future. Thurman and Berner point out that, although monetary and fiscal policy can pass on to future generations the real burden of the income transfer to oil-rich nations, no macroeconomic policy can eliminate this burden.

The results of the analysis by Mork and Hall suggest that policies that encourage capital formation offer an easier choice between inflation and unemployment. Specifically, cutting payroll taxes and providing tax incentives for new investment seem to have this potential. These suggestions apparently reflect the current ideas of many economists, including those who do not accept the assumptions underlying Mork and Hall's policy analysis.

Goettle discusses policy alternatives for the supply side of the economy. Specifically, he discusses alternative measures for reducing the nation's dependence on foreign oil. Of the alternatives he considers, he finds the net social cost to be substantially lower for an energy conservation program than for an accelerated development of synthetic and unconventional fuels. However, the conservation program turns out to be economically inferior to the third alternative of no new policy. Goettle's findings provide an important supplement to the policy analyses discussed above: Although the short-run adjustment problems after an energy price shock may be eased by proper choice of macroeconomic policy, there is little that can be done to improve on the consequences for long-term economic growth.

But in a sense this is good news. For, although little can be done about the long-run problems, they are not quite as painful because the economy can adjust to them. The pain is experienced in the short run, in the form of lost jobs and inefficient use of the nation's resources, as well as unexpected inflation.

It is the hope of this editor that the results presented in the following chapters can be useful to policymakers in their attempts to alleviate some of this pain.

2 ENERGY PRICES, ECONOMIC ACTIVITY, AND INFLATION
A Survey of Issues and Results

*Robert S. Dohner**

I. INTRODUCTION

No postwar events have so colored the macroeconomic horizon as those in the world oil market in the aftermath of the October 1973 Arab-Israeli war. The reduction in oil production by the Organization of Petroleum Exporting Countries (OPEC) in November and December and the embargo on shipments to the United States and the Netherlands created the first "oil crisis"—the prospect of a significant shortfall in available oil supplies. The supply crisis was short-lived, but far more important and enduring in its effects was the quadrupling of oil prices at the beginning of 1974. Although other forces also contributed to the economic turmoil that followed, higher OPEC oil prices helped push the industrialized countries into the sharpest recession since the 1930s. Reviewing the 1974–1975 recession in the United States, one forecaster concludes: "The energy crisis was the single largest cause of the ... recession. Without it the economy would have suffered through no worse than a year of a

*Assistant Professor, Fletcher School of Law and Diplomacy, Tufts University. The views expressed here are those of the author and do not necessarily reflect those of Tufts University, the Fletcher School of Law and Diplomacy, or the M.I.T. Energy Laboratory. I would like to thank Benjamin J. Cohen, Richard Mancke, Knut A. Mork, and David Munro for helpful comments. Nicholas Ronalds provided research assistance. Financial support from the M.I.T. Center for Energy Policy Research is gratefully acknowledged.

small GNP [Gross National Product] decline in 1974, and would have seen 1975 as the first year of recovery." (Eckstein 1978, p. 124).

The sharp rise in oil prices in 1974 imposed difficult adjustment problems upon the consuming countries, problems qualitatively different from those previously faced. After Keynes, the emphasis in macroeconomic policy had been on demand management; one could assure full employment and reasonable stability of prices, it was hoped, by holding aggregate demand near, but not too near, the steadily growing productive capacity of the economy. Although many of the effects of the oil price increase were recognized at the time, it fit badly in this framework. The quadrupling of the oil price was referred to alternately as "inflationary" and "deflationary"—at the same time tending to increase prices and to lower the level of economic activity, producing the anomaly of accelerating inflation and rising unemployment.[1] Economic policymakers faced the difficult choice of exercising restraint to try to moderate domestic rates of price increase, or of trying to maintain levels of employment and economic activity, at the risk of even higher rates of inflation. Although attempts were made in Sweden and the United Kingdom to "accommodate" the oil price increases and maintain employment, most of the nations of the Organization for Economic Cooperation and Development (OECD) opted for restraint, resulting in the deepest postwar recession.[2]

The oil-consuming nations experienced a second sharp rise in OPEC prices in June 1979, in the wake of the Iranian Revolution. Although the increase was not as great in percentage terms as that of 1974, it came on top of a very sluggish recovery in Europe and Japan and a higher underlying rate of inflation in the United States.

In the intervening five years considerable theoretical and econometric effort has been expended to understand and to model the effects of oil or—more generally—energy price increases.[3] The most fruitful approach has been to consider energy as a primary input in production, and to divorce the energy-producing sector in a country, if there is one, from the larger goods- and services-producing sector. The analysis then concentrates on the effects of a rise in the price of energy *relative* to the price of output from the goods and services sector. This has implications for the income of nonenergy factors of production and for aggregate demand, as discussed below. But many of the effects come through induced changes in production techniques and costs, which are the determinants of aggregate supply.

For this reason, energy price increases and similar events have commonly been referred to as "supply shocks" in recent macroeconomic literature.

The following chapters of this volume report the results of several attempts to analyze and quantify the effects of energy price changes on the macroeconomy. This chapter surveys the issues involved in this analysis as well as the results of some of the attempts to quantify the macroeconomic effects of the 1973–1974 oil price increase on the U.S. economy. Section II gives an overview of the events in the world oil market over the last decade. Section III discusses a simple framework, similar to the ones presented in current textbooks, for analyzing aggregate supply and demand. This framework is used to distinguish the effects of a rise in foreign oil prices from the effects of a general foreign inflation. Sections IV and V investigate the effects of energy price increases on aggregate demand and supply, respectively. Section VI deals with the effects of energy price increases on inflation. Finally, Section VII reviews various estimates of the effects of the 1974 rise in oil prices. Section VIII presents some overall conclusions.

II. EVENTS IN THE WORLD MARKET[4]

As a result of the October War in 1973 and the American decision to supply Israel with arms (Lenczowski 1975), the Arab oil producers declared an embargo on oil exports to the United States. The Netherlands was also placed under embargo. Production was to be curtailed as well; November output was finally set at 75 percent of the September level. In December, production was raised, and in March, the Arab oil ministers agreed to end the embargo of shipments to the United States and to restore production to pre-October levels. The embargo on shipments to the Netherlands was lifted in July.

The reduction in Arab oil production was offset only slightly by increases from other producing areas. Despite this and the direction of the embargo against the United States, this country fared reasonably well during the October to March period. The embargo could not be enforced for tankers at sea, and the oil companies were able to redirect supplies from non-Arab producing countries to the United States. A reduction in crude-oil imports began to be felt in December, and the volume of imports reached a low in February

of 60 percent of its October level. U.S. imports of petroleum products—coming mainly from non-Arab countries—were scarcely affected by the embargo (Perry 1975b, Table 2–1, p. 75).

Since about three-quarters of U.S. oil demand was being met by
domestic supply at the time, oil consumption in this country was not
affected much by the embargo. Petroleum consumption in the first
quarter of 1974 was down by only 7 percent from a year earlier, a
considerably smaller decline than in most European countries (Stobaugh 1975, p. 192). Actions by the Federal Energy Office shifted
the brunt of the shortfall to gasoline consumption, although the distribution of the hardship, as measured by the length of gasoline lines,
varied markedly by state. The consumption decline may have exaggerated the extent of the supply shortfall; an exceptionally warm
winter helped, and by April the stocks of almost every petroleum
product had increased considerably (Mancke 1975, p. 4).

The 1978–1979 Oil Crisis[5]

Events in Iran in late 1978 confronted the consuming countries with
the prospect of a second shortfall of oil production. Perceptions of
the vulnerability of the Shah's regime spread in the latter half of the
year, and oil companies began adding to their stocks of oil in anticipation of a possible reduction in supply. This anticipation turned out
to be correct as Iranian oil production dropped during the ensuing
turmoil, and oil exports were suspended entirely in January and February 1979. The fear of a prolonged shortage sparked pressure on
spot markets, where prices soared. Iranian oil production eventually
resumed in the second quarter, but at a level roughly 30 percent below that of the first nine months of 1978.

Iran had been the world's second largest exporter of crude oil, and
was responsible for about 15 percent of the world oil trade in 1978.
However, although the effect of the cessation of Iranian exports on
the world oil market was considerable, production increases in other
countries (especially Saudi Arabia, Iraq, the United Kingdom, and
Nigeria) moderated the effect on world oil supplies. Data from the
Oil and Gas Journal[6] show that total production in noncommunist
countries fell by only 4.3 percent from the fourth quarter of 1978 to
the first quarter of 1979, and regained its previous level in the second
quarter. A relatively minor drop in the available supply of oil was

worsened by speculative buying and stockpiling and, in the United States, by regulations that precluded access to more expensive supplies.[7] The visible effects of the reduction in Iranian oil production were much smaller than for the 1973–1974 oil embargo, but lengthy gasoline lines developed in some sections of the country, particularly in New York City and California.

Oil Prices

While oil shortages slowed economic activity somewhat in the consuming countries, these slowdowns were small and temporary. The major problem turned out to be not the shortages but the dramatic increases in the price of oil. The higher prices persisted after the shortages were gone and confronted the oil-consuming economies with profound and painful adjustment problems.

Calculating crude-oil prices in the late 1950s and the 1960s is a difficult exercise. Posted oil prices were used primarily for determining producer government taxes, and did not generally reflect transaction prices for OPEC oil. Estimates by Adelman (1972) show both crude- and heavy-fuel-oil prices falling steadily from the mid-1950s to 1970.[8] With moderate inflation in the industrial countries, this would mean imported-oil prices fell somewhat more in real terms. One can construct an index of the relative price of delivered energy for the United States by dividing the wholesale price index for fuels, power, and related products by the deflator for the Gross National Product (GNP). This index shows that the relative price of energy fell by 17 percent from 1956–1960 to 1966–1970.

Although the most dramatic increase in world oil prices occurred in the first quarter of 1974, the price of oil had already risen substantially by that time. From December 1970 to October 1973, the posted price of Saudi Arabian light crude oil increased from $1.80 to $5.12, and the Saudi Arabian receipts on crude-oil production are estimated to have jumped from $0.88 to $3.05 per barrel (Darmstadter and Landsberg 1975, p. 26). The explanation for this price rise and the shift in the balance of power away from the companies and toward OPEC has been analyzed elsewhere (Darmstadter and Landsberg 1975 and Penrose 1975). Important factors were the growth of import demand in the consuming countries and, in particular, the exhaustion of spare productive capacity in the United States.

In December 1973, during the embargo, the OPEC ministers met in Tehran and announced that the posted price of Saudi Arabian light crude for January 1974 would be raised to $11.65 a barrel.[9] Subsequent revisions raised posted prices to $13.34 in early 1979. After Iranian oil production resumed, OPEC ministers met in Geneva and announced that, effective July 1, oil prices would be raised to between $18.00 and $23.50 per barrel, depending upon various surcharges. The dispersion of crude-oil prices was substantial, with Saudi Arabian oil selling at $18.00, Kuwait's at about $19.50, Iran's at $22.20, and the African light crudes at about $23.50.[10] Later attempts to achieve a unified OPEC price have been unsuccessful. The Saudi Arabians raised the price of their oil to $24.00 in December 1979. Other producers were free to set their own prices, and some reached $30.

Using the posted price of Saudi Arabian light crude oil as a rough indicator of world oil prices (it understates prices in the second half of 1979), and export unit values of industrial countries as a rough index of the price of their products, Figure 2-1 shows the movement of the relative price of oil from 1972 to 1979. The index rises at the end of 1973, then reaches a peak in the first quarter of 1974. During the next five years the index falls, due both to inflation in the industrial countries and to depreciation of the dollar, although the 1975 appreciation of the dollar relative to other industrial country currencies reversed, for a time, the decline in the relative price. In 1979 the deterioration of the relative price of oil ends, and the index jumps sharply upward.

The price of oil relative to the price of manufactured goods appears to be the central concern of OPEC pricing policy. This concern goes back at least to January 1972, when OPEC increased posted prices by 8.59 percent to compensate for the 1971 devaluation of the dollar, with a second revision in June 1973 after the second devaluation of the dollar (Penrose 1975, pp. 44, 46).

In the period since the 1974 price rise, the OPEC ministers have repeatedly warned the industrial countries that failure to control their rates of inflation would lead to further increases in the price of oil. As the oil minister from Kuwait told a Western audience before the 1979 Geneva meetings, "It is not to your benefit or to ours to see the real price of oil fall."[11]

Figure 2-1.   Posted price of Saudi Arabian crude oil relative to industrial country export unit value index in U.S. dollars (1972 = 1.00).

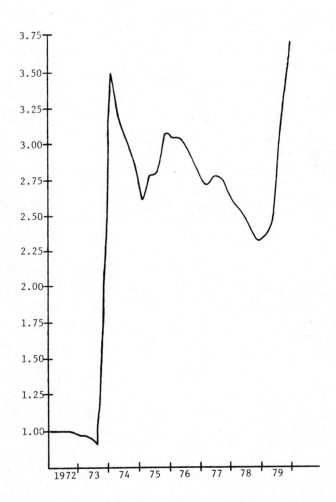

Source: International Monetary Fund. 1979. *International Financial Statistics Yearbook.*

III. ENERGY PRICES IN A MACRO MODEL: AGGREGATE SUPPLY AND DEMAND

The effects of general changes in foreign prices have been analyzed in a variety of macroeconomic models with international linkages. By various mechanisms, an increase in foreign prices is translated into increases in domestic prices and a greater demand for domestic goods and services, and so inflation is transmitted internationally. There was some tendency to view the oil price increase of 1974 in this framework, leading to recommendations of restrictive policies to counter the external, inflationary impulse. A rise in the price of oil is, however, qualitatively different from a general foreign inflation. The difference is easy to see in the framework of a simple aggregate supply-and-demand model, as developed in a number of textbooks in macroeconomics.[12]

Figure 2–2 graphs an aggregate demand curve and an aggregate supply curve. They are similar to the demand and supply curves in a single market but refer to demand and supply of domestic output as a whole. The aggregate demand curve shows demand for domestic output falling with a rise in the price level. This occurs for a number of reasons. With a given supply of money, an increase in the price level lowers the supply of money in real terms, raising interest rates and lowering interest-sensitive components of aggregate demand. The rise in the price level also lowers the real value of the public's wealth, and this may reduce its desired expenditure. Finally, with given prices for foreign goods, an increase in domestic prices makes domestic goods less attractive and foreign goods more attractive, shifting demand (of both domestic residents and foreigners) away from domestic goods.

With fixed input prices, an individual firm has a marginal cost curve (supply curve) that slopes upward as diminishing returns to additional variable inputs are encountered. For the economy as a whole, if variable input costs (wage rates and the prices of energy and materials) are given, the aggregate supply curve shows the prices necessary to bring forth various levels of output from the economy's fixed capital stock. A higher price leads to a higher output, greater employment of labor, and greater use of energy.

It is important to note that the aggregate supply curve is drawn with fixed input costs; if costs rise, then the price necessary to call forth a given level of output must rise in proportion, and the aggre-

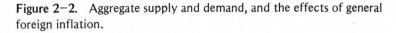

Figure 2–2. Aggregate supply and demand, and the effects of general foreign inflation.

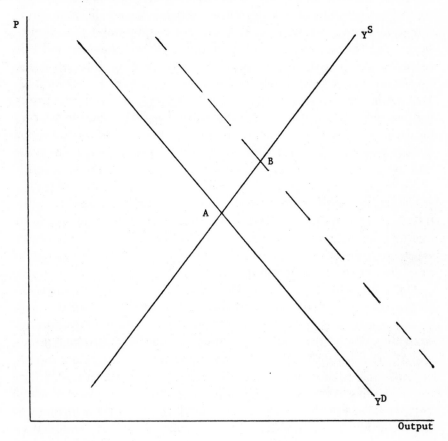

gate supply curve shifts up. For this reason there is a dynamic mechanism associated with the aggregate supply curve, which may cause it to shift over time. If output rises, so does employment, creating an upward pressure on wages, which are part of costs; and vice versa—if output falls, both employment and wages decline relative to what they would have been otherwise.

Figure 2-2 also shows the effect of a general increase in foreign prices. The aggregate supply curve is unaffected by a rise in the prices of foreign goods,[13] but the aggregate demand curve shifts to the right. This is so because higher foreign prices make domestic goods more attractive and foreign goods less attractive, shifting demand by residents and by foreigners toward domestic goods. This increases aggregate demand at any domestic price level, which is captured by the rightward shift of the aggregate demand curve. The new short-run equilibrium is at point B, with a higher output and higher domestic prices. The increase in output reduces unemployment, and this causes wages to rise. Rising wages lead to rising production costs, causing the aggregate supply curve to move upward in Figure 2-2. The upward movement of the aggregate supply curve will raise prices further and lower output (along the shifted aggregate demand curve) until output returns to normal levels and pressure from the labor market subsides. Thus a general rise in foreign prices leads to an eventual rise in domestic prices, and only a temporary increase in output.

An increase in the price of oil relative to the prices of other traded goods has quite different effects in this framework. These are illustrated in Figure 2-3. Since oil—or more generally, energy—is an input to the production process, costs of production increase at given wage and output levels. Thus, the supply price rises; the aggregate supply curve shifts up in Figure 2-3.

The effects upon aggregate demand are ambiguous, but there are strong reasons for thinking that the net effect is a leftward shift in the aggregate demand curve. First, there is no substitution toward domestic goods unless the prices of competing foreign goods are affected more than domestic prices. Second, if energy use cannot be reduced by very much, spending on energy must rise, so unless total spending is increased, expenditure on domestic goods and other imports falls. Finally, as was the case with the 1974 price increase, if the oil producers cannot spend their increased revenues and instead save a large fraction of them, then world demand for the kind of goods the home country produces will fall. The resulting leftward shift in the aggregate demand curve reduces total output and employment, although moderating the rise in prices.

The events shown in Figure 2-3 provide an interesting contrast to the case of a general rise in foreign prices shown in Figure 2-2. An upward shift in the aggregate supply curve increases prices and decreases output and employment, a phenomenon now generally referred to as "stagflation." It is the rise in the relative price of oil that is crucial in this context. If the oil price rise is accompanied by an equal rise in world prices for final goods, then the analysis of Figure 2-2 applies. It is the effect of the relative price change (rise in

Figure 2-3.   A rise in the relative price of imported oil.

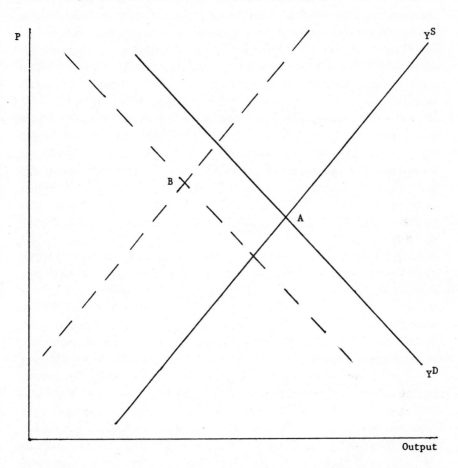

the real price of oil) that will show up throughout the analysis, alter-ing the conclusions of conventional macroeconomic models that use a single commodity price.

IV.   EFFECTS OF AN ENERGY PRICE RISE
UPON AGGREGATE DEMAND

We shall now consider in some detail the effects of an increase in the relative price of energy upon the aggregate demand curve of Fig-ure 2-3. The argument will proceed from a discussion of the effects of the increase upon the income of the other factors of production, to a discussion of the effects upon demand for domestic goods at *any* level of income. We shall look then at effects upon demand due to changes in wealth, and finally at investment and export demand.

In the textbook development of macroeconomics, the circular income-expenditure process is introduced to show that each product sale results in an equal amount of income, divided among the factors of production. In an economy that imports some inputs, such as oil, a part of the income generated goes to foreigners. If the price of the imported input rises relative to that of domestic output, then domestic income falls. The extent of the income drop depends upon the share of the imported input in total costs, as well as the possibilities for substitution away from the imported input. The more substitution, the less is the drop in domestic income.[14]

Although some energy is supplied domestically, a similar analysis may be used for energy inputs to production. For illustration, we may assume that aggregate output is produced by two factors — energy and a composite of labor and capital input. The substitution possibilities can then be described by the elasticity of substitution between the two factors. If this elasticity is zero, the two factors are used in fixed proportions, and no substitution is possible. If it is one, we have the Cobb–Douglas production function with fixed income shares for the two factors. Using data on business energy inputs assembled by George Perry (1978), we find that the ratio of energy use to output declined by 10.2 percent between 1973 and 1976, a period in which the relative price of energy[15] rose by 57 percent. Perry attributes most of the decline in energy use to factors other than substitution (a point discussed below), but if we consider the decline as input substitution, we may observe that payments for energy per unit of output rise by 41 percent, so the implied elasticity of substitution is 0.24.[16] Primary energy costs represented about 4 percent of GNP in 1973, so this would imply that the income received by nonenergy factors per unit of output fell by 1.7 percent. Other estimates of the elasticity of substitution indicate a range of 0.2 to 0.6 (Hogan and Manne 1977, p. 252). With an elasticity of 0.6 and a 57 percent rise in relative energy prices, payments to energy per unit of output would rise only by 20 percent.

If a country produces some of its energy and imports the rest, as is the case in the United States, then part of the increased payments for energy inputs will accrue as income to the domestic energy sector. However, in the United States, price controls for domestically produced fuels have limited the extent of this internal redistribution of income. This policy has had some important unfortunate consequences. By averaging in the higher cost of foreign oil with the generally controlled U.S. energy prices, the price control policy served as a disincentive to substituting away from energy use and as an incentive to buying more foreign energy.[17]

Thus, the first effect of the rise in energy prices was to lower the income received by domestic factors of production at any level of total production. In addition, that income, or share in total value of domestic goods production, now represented a lower real income when measured in terms of a basket of goods that included direct consumption of energy as well as domestic goods. The real income effect of the rise in energy prices would tend to decrease the quantities demanded of both goods. On the other hand, the energy price rise also creates a substitution effect away from energy and toward domestic goods. If, as appears likely, the substitution effect is small, then consumer demand for domestic goods will fall after the price change.[18]

However, expenditures on domestic goods and expenditures on energy are not the only alternatives for disposal of income. Part of income is saved, and changes in savings may absorb some of the effects of the relative price change. A reduction in current savings may support expenditures, either because the proportion of income saved rises with real income (Laursen and Metzler 1950), or because it takes some time for consumption patterns to adjust, so consumption is financed by lower savings in the adjustment period. It is difficult to disentangle this effect from the cyclical effects depressing consumption, but it may have occurred after the energy price rises in 1979. Table 2–1 shows personal consumption expenditures on energy, expenditures on other goods and services, and personal savings, as percentages of personal disposable income. As Table 2–1 indicates, about half of the 0.8 percentage point increase in the share of energy expenditures in personal disposable income came from a decline in the share of nonenergy expenditures, and half came from a reduction in the share of savings. The reduction of savings moderated the effects of the energy price increase in reducing nonenergy consumption demand.

These are the main effects that occur through the income-expenditure channel. Several macroeconomic models also emphasize the

Table 2–1.   Disposition of personal disposable income[a] 1976–1979 (*in percentages*).

	1976	1977	1978	1979
Personal savings	5.9	5.1	5.1	4.7
Energy consumption[b]	7.6	7.7	7.6	8.4
Nonenergy consumption	86.5	87.2	87.4	87.0

Source: *Economic Report of the President*, 1980, and *Survey of Current Business*, various issues.

a. Personal disposable income less interest payments and transfers.

b. Expenditures for gasoline and oil, fuel oil and coal, and electricity and gas.

effects of changes in real wealth upon consumption. If the prices of other factors of production do not fall, then a rise in energy prices increases the general price level, as prices of energy use rise, and as additional energy costs are passed through in the prices of other products. This causes asset holdings of the public to fall in real terms, lowering the wealth, and therefore the expenditures, of domestic consumers. The rise in price may also severely affect the liquidity of consumers, causing a further retrenchment of expenditures. The "consumer balance sheet" as a determinant of expenditure is examined by Mishkin (1977), who finds that it explains a significant proportion of the decline in expenditure, particularly for consumer durables, during the 1974–1975 recession.

The other important components of aggregate demand are investment demand and export demand; a rise in energy prices will have effects on both. Investment demand, or demand for additions to the capital stock, depends upon the return to capital (the marginal product of capital) relative to the returns available on other assets (the interest rate or rates). In the goods and services sector, the effect on investment demand depends on the characteristics of the production process. An additional unit of capital will be more valuable and investment demand will be greater if capital can be substituted for energy in production (capital-energy substitutability). If capital use is associated with energy use, so that additional capital requires additional energy (capital-energy complementarity), then a rise in the price of energy discourages capital use as well as energy use, resulting in a decrease in investment demand.

Whether capital and energy are substitutes or complements is an unsettled empirical question, and one that has important implications for short-run aggregate demand and medium-term economic growth. Econometric analyses have split on the question,[19] while engineering studies of industrial processes indicate substantial possibilities for substitution.[20] One plausible explanation is that energy and capital are substitutes at the design stage, whereas energy and existing capital are complements. If this is the case, then the effects of a rise in the price of energy on investment demand will not be so severe, and investment might even increase if the replacement of the existing capital stock is accelerated.[21] Unfortunately, our experience with higher energy prices may as yet be too brief to provide precise answers concerning capital demand.

Accelerated investment in the domestic energy sector may also help maintain aggregate investment activity. If the relative price of energy increases, then the returns to factors employed in the energy sector will increase. Although real, nonresidential fixed investment fell by 0.3 percent in the United States in 1974 and by 14 percent in 1975, real investment in the petroleum industry rose by 32 percent and by 14 percent in each of the two years, respectively.[22]

The last determinant of investment demand is the opportunity cost of investable funds, or the interest rate. The interest rate will depend on the increased demand for (nominal) money due to higher prices, the level of income, and the monetary policy of the authorities. As discussed below, the Federal Reserve restricted monetary growth after the oil price increases, so interest rates rose sharply in 1974, further discouraging investment demand.

A final source of demand for domestic goods and services comes from foreigners' demand for domestic exports. If we divide the world into two types of countries, oil-importing countries and oil-exporting countries, then a rise in the relative price of oil lowers real income in the importing countries and raises it in the exporting countries. The fall in real income in the oil-importing countries lowers demand in those countries, and lowers the importing countries' demand for each others exports. By the same token, part of the increase in real income in the oil-exporting countries leads to additional demand for imported goods in those countries. If goods and energy are consumed in the same proportions in oil-exporting and oil-importing countries, and if the substitution effects caused by the relative price change are weak, then the net effect on demand for oil-importing country output depends upon whether world expenditure rises or falls. If, as is probably the case, the savings propensity is higher in the oil-exporting countries than in the oil-importing countries, then world expenditure demand will fall with the real-income transfer, and demand for the output of oil-importing countries will fall as well.

This characterization describes the pattern of industrial country exports in 1974, in the wake of the oil price increases. GATT estimates that the volume of industrial country exports rose by about 7.5 percent in 1974, about one-half of the rate of increase of the previous year.[23] However, the volume of mutual trade among the industrialized countries rose by only 1 percent, whereas industrial country export volumes to the oil-exporting countries increased by about 30 percent. During the recession of 1975, exports of the industrial countries fell by about 4 percent, mostly due to a decline in trade among themselves.[24]

A change in the relative price of oil makes interpretation of trade balances tricky. Industrial country trade balances deteriorated substantially in 1974 and again in 1979 when measured in nominal terms, but improved significantly if measured in constant prices. The identification of this "real" improvement as a net stimulus to aggregate demand is difficult, for it was not an independent stimulus, but rather a result of the income transfer from oil-importing to oil-exporting nations.[25]

Two additional, policy-determined factors that played a role in the 1974–1975 recession merit mention. The first is the behavior of the money stock, and the second is the effect of the price rises via the progressive tax system. To combat what was seen as an inflationary shock to the economy, monetary growth slowed in 1974. As a result, the real value (in terms of the consumer price index) of the broadly defined money stock, M2, fell by 4 percent from the fourth quarter of 1973 to the fourth quarter of 1974. Interest rates rose to record levels in mid-1974, and the demand for investment goods, particularly housing, was severely affected. Inflation rates hit 11 percent in 1974, raising nominal, although not real, incomes. This forced many taxpayers into higher tax brackets and, due to the progressiveness of the income tax system, raised the proportion of income taken in taxes. Federal receipts rose 12.6 percent from the calendar year 1973 to 1974, compared to an 8.1 percent increase in nominal GNP and a 1.4 percent fall in real GNP. Personal income tax receipts rose by 15 percent, although personal taxable income rose by only 8 percent.[26] This increase in the proportion of income taxed was the result of inflation and exerted a substantial drag on aggregate demand.

V. AGGREGATE SUPPLY, PRODUCTIVITY, AND GROWTH

The existing empirical evidence strongly suggests that prices are determined, even in the short run, by a fairly constant markup over unit costs.[27] If energy prices rise and other input prices do not fall, then domestic product prices will rise, on a first approximation by the proportion of energy in total costs. Robert Gordon (1975b) has estimated the effects of the energy price increases on U.S. product prices. He finds the rise in energy prices raises the deflator for private final sales by 1.3 percent from the fourth quarter of 1973 to the second quarter of 1974; and by 2.6 percent from the fourth quarter of 1973 to the third quarter of 1975. This increase in prices shifts the aggregate supply curve upward in Figure 2–3. If wages rise as a result of energy price increases (due to indexing, or for other reasons described below), then the upward shift of the aggregate supply curve will be magnified.

The change in relative factor prices alters the desired input proportions, factor productivity, and even desired output. If production processes allow some substitution of other inputs when energy becomes more expensive, then the productivity of those other inputs will fall. We will concentrate on labor, because the capital stock is largely fixed in the short run, and because the possibilities for substituting capital for energy appear to be limited in the short run as well. At a given level of output, with a rise in energy prices, the firm will substitute labor for energy inputs if possible. This will lower the average productivity of labor, since more labor is now being used to produce the same volume of output. The substitution is also likely to lower the marginal product of labor, because the supply of other inputs is now spread more thinly across the labor employed, and each laborer has less of the other inputs to work with. For this reason, one would expect the equilibrium (full employment) wage to fall in terms of the price of the domestic product.

The extent of substitution possibilities and the effect of the rise in energy prices on labor demand and labor productivity are areas of recent controversy. Rasche and Tatom (1977b) have made a case for considerable substitutability of labor and energy in production, and therefore for a sizable impact on labor demand and labor productivity. Rasche and Tatom estimate a Cobb–Douglas production function for the output of the U.S. private business sector in terms of inputs of capital, labor, and energy. The estimated share parameters are 0.65 for labor and 0.12 for energy. Since the share of each factor in total costs is constant for the Cobb–Douglas function, substantial substitutability is imposed by the function chosen. From 1972 to 1976 the price of energy relative to labor rose by 68 percent; this would indicate an increase in labor demand at a constant level of output of about 8.5 percent, and a corresponding fall in the average product of labor.[28]

The conclusions of Rasche and Tatom of considerable substitution possibilities for energy and the substantial effect of a rise in energy prices on productivity have been challenged by Perry (1978) and Denison (1979). The challenges have been on two grounds. Rasche and Tatom did not have information on energy inputs, and instead used an equilibrium energy demand relationship involving relative prices. The 12 percent estimate of energy's share in total costs is much higher than the 4 to 5 percent that others have found. This would overstate the effect on labor demand. Cost shares of 0.70 for labor and 0.05 for energy would imply an increase in labor demand at constant output of only 3.8 percent. Perry and Denison also argue that the Cobb–Douglas function overstates the degree of substitutability between labor and energy.

As indicated above, Perry (1978) found a decline in energy use per unit of output of 10.2 percent between 1973 and 1976, coupled with a relative price increase of 57 percent. Perry estimated the trend of business energy use per unit of output from 1949 to 1973, then attributed one-half to two-thirds of the 10 percent reduction as due to that trend. Much of the rest he attributed to elimination of nonproductive energy use, and he concludes that possibilities for substitution away from energy toward labor are quite limited.

The calculation of energy input is an important step, but Perry may err in his calculation of the trend effect. A series perhaps comparable to Perry's—the ratio of energy use per unit of output in manufacturing—is examined by Alterman (1977). Alterman adjusts his data for shifts in industrial activity among industries with more and less intensive use of energy. Using a fixed weight index for five energy-intensive industries (accounting for about 80 percent of the energy consumed in manufacturing), he finds that energy use per unit of output rose by 0.2 percent per year between 1967 and 1971, then fell by 2.9 percent per year between 1971 and 1974 (1977, p. 81, Table 21). This coincides roughly with the movements in the relative price of energy, but the variations in price are much larger. The relative price of energy reached its low point in 1970, increased by 9 percent between 1970 and 1973, and by an additional 42 percent in 1974. The interpretation of this evidence is not clear. It does suggest that substitution possibilities are considerably less than those implied by the Cobb–Douglas function, but it also suggests that the relevant constant-energy-price trend may be difficult to determine.

Other econometric estimates indicate some possibilities for substitution. Berndt and Wood (1975) estimate a long-run partial elasticity of substitution between labor and energy of 0.65, which, if energy's share in costs was 5 percent, would indicate an increase in labor demand per unit of output of 1.7 percent.[29] Hudson and Jorgenson (1978b), using a sectoral model that emphasizes energy, find that real GNP fell by 3.2 percent from 1972 to 1976 due to the increase in prices, while labor demand declined by only 0.6 percent. The increase in labor demand per unit of output comes from two sources— the substitution of labor for energy in each sector and the shift in final demand away from energy-intensive and toward labor-intensive industries.

Whatever the extent of energy price–induced substitution of labor, there has been a clear recent break in the trend of labor input per unit of output. This is usually examined in terms of its reciprocal, output per unit of labor, or labor productivity. Denison (1979) reviews postwar productivity growth. From 1947 to 1973, national income per person employed grew at an average rate of 2.43 percent per year. Between 1973 and 1976, it fell at an annual rate of 0.54 percent—an unprecedented drop. Furthermore, this abrupt drop in productivity growth seems to have characterized all industrialized countries (1979, p. 20, Table 3). The break in productivity growth seems also to have occurred in one year: "According to my estimates there is no unexplained retardation in the rate of growth of productivity until 1974, and the drop in the rate that started at that time was abrupt and large. I consider this timing an important clue in any attempt to unravel the mystery surrounding the productivity slowdown" (1979, p. 5).

Denison rejects the rise in energy prices as an explanation for the reversal in productivity growth, based largely upon the evidence in Perry (1978). I do not find this evidence conclusive, and consider the matter still an open question.

Since greater substitutability of labor for energy in production involves a greater fall in labor productivity, one may be tempted to conclude that substitutability hurts. This conclusion is incorrect: Substitution leads to lower production costs and a reduction in payments to (largely foreign) energy. When the price of energy—or any other nonlabor input—increases, it is desirable to use more labor to produce the same output.

The substitution of labor for energy also plays an important social role by cushioning the unemployment effects of the fall in output. Rasche and Tatom (1977a) and others have noted that employment recovered much faster from the 1974—1975 recession than in previous ones. This is an indication that labor substitution, with some lag, alleviated the unemployment effects of the recession.

If firms use less energy to produce their output, the level of total output with full employment of other factors (labor, capital) will be reduced. If one defines potential output as the output of profit-maximizing firms when all domestic resources are fully employed, then potential output falls as a result of the increase in the relative price of energy.

Calculations of potential or "high employment" output have conventionally been made using an empirical relationship between employment and the rate of growth of output known as Okun's law. Substitution in production would alter the relationship between labor and output and thus affect the calculation of potential output. This would have important implications for analyzing fiscal policy, since fiscal policy is usually evaluated by government expenditures and receipts at *potential* output, rather than at current output. It would also have important implications for determining how close the economy is to full utilization, and therefore to inflation—although in this case the rate of unemployment remains an alternative, and perhaps preferable, measure.

Rasche and Tatom (1977a) and Perry (1978) examine the issue of potential output and reach opposing conclusions. Rasche and Tatom find potential output increased by only 6 percent from 1973 as compared to an 11 percent rise in the corresponding measure of the Council of Economic Advisers (1977a, p. 20). Perry finds essentially no change in the estimate of potential output due to the rise in energy prices, since, for the reasons reviewed above, he finds essentially no substitution away from energy.

The medium- and long-term effects on the growth of potential output depend on what happens to capital. As discussed above, an increase in the relative price of energy seems likely to lead to a fall in the demand for investment, but the extent of the decline is influenced by the degree of substitutability or complementarity. If investment slackens and the labor force continues to grow, the labor intensity of production will increase. This will raise the marginal product of capital and raise investment demand. Thus, investment will recover from a rise in energy prices, but only after a period of slow growth in output and productivity. If there is no future change in the relative price of energy, then the previous rate of output growth will be restored. Models that assume a rising real price of energy (e.g., Hudson and Jorgenson 1978a) produce a permanently lowered output growth rate.

VI. EFFECTS ON INFLATION

If wages and other factor returns are completely flexible, then the general price level need not be affected by a change in the relative price of energy. Other factor returns could fall sufficiently to allow product prices to fall, maintaining the level of a composite price index. If other prices do not fall, then a rise in the relative price of energy can only be accomplished through a rise in the general price level. Much of the extraordinarily high rate of inflation in 1974 and 1975 can be described in this fashion as an adjustment to the rise in world oil prices in 1974.[30]

If the rise in the relative price of energy takes place in an already inflationary environment, one could draw a logical distinction between the rise in the general price level that reflects the relative price change, and the change in the price level due to general inflation. In practice it may be difficult to maintain this distinction, for the cost increases caused by the rise in energy prices may take some time to completely pass through to the prices of other goods. The price of direct uses of energy (such as gasoline) and prices of goods with a very high energy content (petrochemicals and fertilizer) would rise quickly. Prices of other goods might respond more slowly, particularly to the increased energy costs of intermediate inputs. Increases in costs in the production of capital goods would be the slowest to pass through into costs of final goods.

The adjustment time also would depend upon how quickly energy prices rose to energy users. For the industrial countries as a whole, from Figure 2-1, the relative price of oil rose very quickly, reaching a peak in the first quarter of 1974. In the United States, prices paid for energy did not rise by the full extent of the OPEC price increase, because price controls on domestic oil and gas production kept prices down and because rate hearing processes delayed the increase in electricity prices. Over time, average prices for energy increased as cost passthroughs in electric generation were allowed, as price controls on natural-gas production were relaxed, as more of U.S. oil production passed into uncontrolled categories, and as the United States imported a higher fraction of its total energy use. The recent decontrol of domestic oil prices has also added to increased energy costs in the United States.

An index of the relative price of energy in the United States (the wholesale price index for fuels and power divided by the GNP deflator) is shown in Figure 2-4. In contrast to the relative price of oil for the industrial countries shown in Figure 2-1, the relative price of energy in the United States rose continuously throughout the period. This led to a protracted adjustment in the United States, and a higher measured rate of inflation in the latter half of the 1970s.[31]

One can still distinguish between the adjustment inflation, as the price of energy rises relative to other prices, and the underlying rate of inflation in the general price index. The interesting and crucial question is whether the rise in the relative price of energy affects the underlying rate of inflation so that an inflationary legacy remains after the adjustment in relative prices takes place.[32]

The evidence of cost-determined pricing and the predominance of labor costs in total costs has led inflation theory to concentrate on the labor market. In his celebrated article, A.W. Phillips found an inverse relationship between the unemployment rate and the rate of wage increase in the United Kingdom. The theoretical foundations of the Phillips curve were refined by Edmund Phelps and Milton Friedman, who argued that real, and not nominal, wages were at issue in the process of bargaining and wage determination. Unemployment might affect the path of wages, but if a certain increase in

Figure 2–4.   Relative price of energy in the United States.[a]

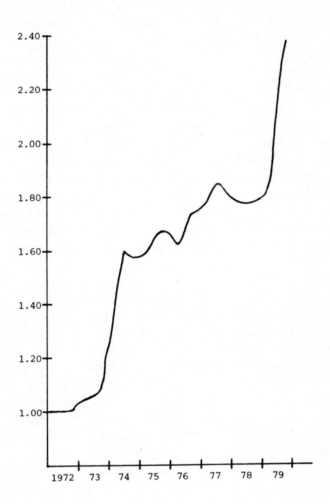

Source: Survey of Current Business, various issues.
a. Wholesale price index for fuels and power, divided by the GNP deflator, 1972 = 1.00.

the price level was expected to occur, then workers would demand, and employers be willing to grant, an equivalent increase in wages.

In a simple macroeconomic model with a single commodity price, there is no difficulty in defining "the real wage." A rise in energy prices complicates the definition, for the energy price increase is a change in relative prices, which introduces at least two goods into the real-wage definition.

The domestic producer is interested in the cost of labor relative to the sales value of the production that an additional laborer represents. For him the real wage is defined in terms of the price of output of the goods and services sector. Since a rise in relative energy prices leads to an increased share of energy in production costs, the producer will require a fall in the real wage, defined in terms of output prices, to maintain a given level of employment.

In contrast, the wage earner is concerned with the real wage defined in terms of the goods he buys, a signficant proportion of which are direct purchases of energy. With a rise in the price of energy relative to domestic output prices, the wage will have to rise relative to output prices if a constant consumption real wage is to be maintained.

To illustrate this point, consider the price changes that occurred in the United States. Between 1973 and 1974, the implicit deflator for personal consumption expenditures (a consumption price index) rose by 10.8 percent, while the GNP deflator (a domestic product price index) rose only 9.7 percent, a difference of only 1.2 percentage points. If no substitution away from energy is assumed, it is possible to net out the increased production expenditure for energy, as Robert Gordon (1975b) does. His deflator net of energy (a measure of what could be paid other factors) rises by 8.7 percent between 1973 and 1974, or by 2.1 percentage points less than the consumption price deflator.

The way in which wages respond to an energy price rise is crucial in determining whether the underlying rate of inflation is affected by the relative price change. If wages rise less quickly than output prices, reflecting the decline in labor productivity caused by higher energy prices, then the adjustment may take place without a change in the underlying inflation rate. If the rate of wage increase rises—particularly if it rises in response to changes in the consumption price index—then a rise in energy prices leads to a round of wage-price inflation. The rise in the relative price of energy reduces the real (consumption) incomes of domestic capital and labor, and there is no way that the real incomes of both can be maintained through wage and rental increases.

Despite this fact, there are reasons to believe that changes in the real wage defined in terms of a consumption price index determine at least a part of nominal wage changes, so an increase in the relative price of energy raises the underlying inflation rate. The most straightforward reason is wage contract indexation, almost all of which is done on the basis of a consumption price index. Of the 9.7 million workers the Labor Department estimates are covered by major collective bargaining agreements, some 5.8 million (60 percent) have contracts with escalator clauses (LeRoy 1978, Table 4). Most cost-of-living adjustments are based on changes in the consumer price index (CPI); the most common is a 1 cent per hour increase for each 0.3 or 0.4 percentage point change in the CPI (1978, p. 7). Outside of major collective bargaining agreements, the use of explicit indexation in the United States is not very common (Braun 1976, p. 268). Indexation is much more widespread and complete in Europe, except in Germany and France, which makes adjustment to a rise in the relative price of energy more difficult.[33]

Even if wage contracts are not explicitly indexed, wages may increase to offset deteriorations in labor's real earnings, even when this is not accompanied by increases in product prices. This could occur because wages in one occupation relative to wages in other occupations are important in the wage-setting process, and the pattern of wages includes contracts that are indexed. Or it could occur simply because the real earnings of labor and their development over time are important issues in the bargaining process. Reductions in labor's real earnings could lead to a push for higher earnings, as Wilkinson and Turner (1972) argue occurred with increases in payroll taxation in the United Kingdom.

If wages rise as a result of higher energy prices, then the aggregate supply curve in Figure 2-3 would shift up further, as increasing wage costs raise the supply price of output. Prices would rise, lowering the real wage, and output would fall, raising unemployment. A wage-price spiral could continue until unemployment and disappointed real-wage expectations reconciled labor to a new, lower real wage. Attempts to raise output and employment by shifting the aggregate demand curve would further raise prices, and might simply prolong the adjustment to an equilibrium real wage.

The empirical evidence on wage adjustment to the oil price rise is mixed. Klein (1978, p. 86) attributes wage increases in Britain and Scandinavia after 1973 to the rise in oil prices. In contrast, Gordon (1977), using lagged changes in a price index net of food and energy, and lagged change in a consumer price index, finds that the consumer price index changes do not help to explain U.S. wage inflation. Gordon concludes: "... *none* of the 1973–74 inflation in food and energy prices 'got into' wages, and all pre-1971 wage equations that allow influences of food and energy prices drastically overpredict the cumulative 1971–76 wage increase" (1977, p. 268).

Branson and Rotemberg (1979) and Sachs (1979) review the course of real wages in the OECD countries after the rise in oil and commodity prices. In contrast to the United States, where the real wage falls between 1973 and 1975, in Europe and Japan the real wage increases beyond what is warranted by declining productivity and increases in the relative prices of other inputs.[34] The fall in real wages in the United States is evidence that the adjustment to higher oil prices has taken place, while this appears not to have happened in Europe and Japan. At various times after 1974, the United States had urged its trading partners to undertake a coordinated expansion that would pull the industrialized countries out of the recession. European and Japanese leaders hesitated, apparently fearing renewed inflation, and these economies have been sluggish or stagnant since 1975. As a result, a strong recovery in the United States ran into external difficulties and a rapidly depreciating dollar in late 1977.

If there is very limited flexibility in real wages in Europe and Japan, then it may be impossible to increase output prices relative to wages and move up along the supply curve in Figure 2–2 or Figure 2–3. In such a case, increases in demand would lead to rapid increases in wages and prices with little or no effect on the level of output. Branson and Rotemberg and Sachs attribute the unwillingness of European and Japanese leaders to participate in a coordinated expansion to this lack of flexibility in the real wage.

VII. ECONOMETRIC MODELING OF
THE 1974–1975 RECESSION

This section describes several attempts to estimate the effects that the steep rise in world oil prices had on the U.S. economy in 1974 and 1975. This is not a comparison of the accuracy of various models, since the estimates were made at different times, on different variables, and with generally differing assumptions. It rather provides a way to gauge the importance of the energy price increase on U.S. economic performance.

The forecasts of major macroeconomic models have been compared by Stephen McNees in a series of articles.[35] In the five models he surveys,[36] forecasts of output and the GNP deflator made one year in advance perform reasonably well until 1974, although the rate of inflation was substantially underestimated in 1973.

The performance of the macroeconomic models deteriorates markedly when forecasts for the first quarter of 1974 through mid-1975 (made one year previously) are examined. Output growth is consistently and greatly overestimated, and inflation is underestimated. This is of course due in large part to the inability to predict the external events of 1973 and 1974, but even in April 1974, after the rise in oil prices and the first quarter fall in GNP were known, the forecasters predicted that GNP growth over the coming year would be between 1.6 and 3.8 percent (it actually fell by 6.1 percent) and inflation would be 6.6 and 8.5 percent (it was actually 11 percent) (McNees 1976, p. 35). After mid-1975, the performance of the forecasts greatly improves, presumably a result of the stabilization of external events and the lessons learned in the previous period.

Modifications of econometric models to include energy price effects have been made by a number of authors, both at the time of the oil price increase and in the period after. The approaches taken by several are summarized here (in chronological order).

Pierce and Enzler (1974) analyze the oil price rise in the M.I.T.–Penn–SSRC (MPS) model. The rise in imported-oil prices and the partial rise in domestic oil prices raise the consumption price deflator by 2 percent relative to the value-added deflator, and raise the latter by 1 percent relative to wages. This lowers real disposable income and wealth and depresses consumption demand. The money demand equation is modified to take into account the additional transactions requirements of higher import prices, leading to a further rise in interest rates. The model is simulated starting with the first quarter of 1967, so the initial conditions do not correspond to those of the other models.

Perry (1975b) analyzes the oil price increases using the Federal Reserve Board and the Michigan econometric models. The increase in oil prices raises the consumption deflator by a total of 3.55 percent relative to its control path, which depresses consumption. An important additional channel affecting consumption is reduced automobile sales. Perry uses the residuals from the automobile demand equation in the Michigan model as an estimate of this effect, and allocates half to other consumption spending and half to increased saving.

Eckstein (1978) analyzed the effects of the energy price increases in the Data Resources, Inc. (DRI), econometric model. The base of comparison is the simulation of the model with actual values of the variables—and with the equation errors added in—so the model tracks history precisely. The effect of the oil price increase is estimated by simulating an alternative scenario where the wholesale price index (WPI) for fuels and power rises by 6 percent per year from early 1973, instead of its actual average of 27.4 percent annual rate of increase in 1973–1975. Eckstein also adds judgmental corrections to gasoline and motor oil expenditures, other nondurable expenditures, and automobile sales.

The econometric model described in Fair (1978) assigns an important role to import prices in the domestic price-wage block. (Holding other variables constant, a 1 percent rise in import prices raises domestic prices by 0.327 percent in the long run.) Instead of looking at the effect of the oil price increases, Fair analyzes what would have happened if import prices had risen by 6 percent per year from the first quarter of 1973 to the fourth quarter of 1974, instead of the average 34.4 percent over the period. About half of the 62 percent increase in import prices between the beginning of 1973 and mid–1974 was due to oil price increases (primarily in 1974), with the other half coming from increases in nonfuel import prices.[37] The Fair paper thus overestimates the effects of the oil price increase.

Mork and Hall (1980b) have estimated a macroeconomic model divided into an energy and a goods and services sector, in the fashion discussed in the previous sections of this chapter. A rise in the price of output of the energy sector lowers the real income of consumers, leading to a permanent drop in their consumption path. A considerable drop in investment contributes importantly to the effects on output in the goods sector. Mork and Hall simulate the effects of the energy price increase experienced in 1974 and 1975 (by 1975 the relative price of primary energy in their model has risen by 94 percent

Table 2–2a. Effects of the 1973–1974 energy price increase in macroeconomic models: real effects.

	Pierce and Enzler MPS	Perry FRB	Perry Michigan	Eckstein DRI	Fair	Mork and Hall
GNP/Output[a]						
1973	–	–	–	−0.3	−0.1	–
1974	−1.2	−2.0	−1.5	−3.2	−1.3	−2.1
1975	−2.8	−3.0	−4.0	−5.7	−5.0	−5.1
1976	−2.1[b]	−2.9	−5.0	–	–	−4.2
1977	−2.0[b]	−3.1	−4.4	–	–	−3.7
Consumption[a]						
1973	–	–	–	−0.5	–	–
1974	−1.6	−2.6	−2.3	−3.1	–	−3.4
1975	−3.4	−3.7	−4.4	−4.7	–	−3.5
1976	−3.6[b]	−4.6	−5.5	–	–	−3.4
1977	−3.9[b]	−5.1	−5.6	–	–	−3.4
Investment[a]						
1973	–	–	–	−0.3	–	–
1974	–	−3.8	−2.3	−2.4	–	−4.0
1975	–	−7.4	−10.8	−10.3	–	−38.2
1976	–	−3.7	−12.4	–	–	−17.5
1977	–	−2.6	−8.5	–	–	−12.8

a. The figures presented are the differences between simulations with energy price rises and control simulations, expressed as a percentage of the actual value of the variable in the year. The Pierce and Enzler simulation starts in 1967, and differences are compared to years 1967-1970. These percentages are then entered as if the simulation began in 1974.

b. Fourth quarter.

and remains at that level), then compare this simulation with a stable growth case with steady 5 percent inflation.

Each author assumes that fiscal and monetary policies are unchanged in the two simulations, but there are some differences in the exact specification of this assumption. Furthermore, each author is forced to make assumptions concerning the behavior of net exports, and these assumptions differ from one author to another. The models also differ in the way the energy price is entered, and the extent of the energy price change. Models without an energy sector (Pierce and Enzler, Perry) raise consumption prices relative to output prices.

Table 2–2b.   Effects of the 1973–1974 energy price increase in macroeconomic models: effects on inflation[a].

	Pierce and Enzler (Consumption Price Def.)	Perry FRB (GNP Def.)	Perry Michigan (GNP Def.)	Eckstein (GNP Def.)	Eckstein (CPI)	Fair (GNP Def.)	Mork and Hall (CPI)
1973	—	—	—	0.5	0.4	1.2	—
1974	2.1	1.3	1.8	1.7	2.6	6.4	4.2
1975	0.8	0.8	2.3	1.9	1.7	6.3	1.8
1976	−0.4[b]	1.1	1.2	—	—	—	0.3
1977	−0.5[b]	1.1	0.0	—	—	—	−0.3

a. Inflation rates are the differences in percentage points between the year-over-year rate of change of the price index in the energy price rise and the control simulations.

b. Fourth-quarter-to-fourth-quarter change.

Models with energy sectors (Eckstein, Mork and Hall) raise or lower an energy price directly. Fair assumes a lower path for import prices. Comparison among the models is further complicated by the fact that the Pierce and Enzler simulation begins in 1967 and by the fact that the output of the goods and services sector in Mork and Hall is slightly different from the GNP measure that the other authors use.

Tables 2–2a and 2–2b collect the simulation results of the studies. To facilitate comparison, changes in real variables are expressed as percentages of the actual value in the relevant year. The Pierce and Enzler results are expressed as percentages of values in 1967 and following years, but moved forward to correspond with the rise in oil prices in 1974. Finally, the gross output of the goods sector, which Mork and Hall use, is compared directly to the GNP figures of the others.

As the table notes, the rise in energy prices (or import prices, in the Fair model) is responsible for a sizable drop in output and an acceleration of inflation. The estimated fall in GNP in 1975 lies in the range of 3 to 5.5 percent in the models surveyed, although the distribution of the drop varies somewhat. The investment sector has a particularly strong role in the Mork–Hall model. The calculated increase in inflation varies widely among the models. Fair, because he uses all import prices, gets a particularly strong response.

Real GNP actually fell by 5.9 percent from its peak quarter in 1973 to its trough in the first quarter of 1975, and year-over-year inflation as measured by the CPI and the GNP deflator rose by 4.7 and 3.9 percentage points, respectively, in 1974. So all of the models surveyed in Tables 2-2a and 2-2b assign a major role to the external price increases.

VIII. CONCLUSIONS

The rise in oil prices imposes difficult adjustment problems because it implies a change in relative prices. The relative price change lowers the real income of the consuming countries, since more of their output is needed to pay for the more expensive oil. This fall in real income must be distributed among domestic factors of production, and if those factors are unwilling to accept a reduction in their real incomes, then inflation and unemployment occur to reconcile the inconsistent claims to the lower national income. The fact that energy use is more expensive affects production decisions, lowering productivity and lowering the level of output when all domestic factors are employed.

If the relative price of oil rises to a higher level and stays there, then the adjustment will be completed eventually. Prices no longer rise due to the rise in the relative price of energy, and incomes begin to grow through investment and technological advance. If the relative price of energy falls due to inflation in the consuming countries, then the adjustment is eased or reversed, until the next round of energy price increases. If the relative importance of energy falls, because of substitution over time away from energy use in production or consumption, then the effects of the rise in the relative price of energy can be permanently moderated.

I will close with a few observations about economic analysis. The oil price change is a difficult analytical problem because it involves a substantial relative price shift. Traditional macroeconomic models do not describe these effects because the aggregation in those models assumes that relative price shifts do not take place. Recent theoretical models by Gordon (1975a), E. Phelps (1978), and Solow (1980), and by Bruno and Sachs (in press) and Dohner (1978) for open economies, have been developed for this purpose, with the substantial impetus of hindsight. Distinctions between output and income, and income and real income, and the precise definition of real magnitudes (for instance, the real wage), are all extremely important.

The change in the relative price also gives reason to distrust the implications of econometric models that have been estimated for periods of near-constancy in relative prices. One example might be the econometric finding of capital-energy complementarity. Since the cost of labor dominated variable production costs over much of the postwar period, techniques may have been developed to substitute labor for capital, with little regard for energy use.[38] Thus, it is not surprising that additional capital use was associated with additional energy use, or that capital and energy would appear as complements in the postwar period. Higher energy prices may well encourage future techniques that will substitute capital for energy. Our experience with higher energy prices is still very brief, too brief to allow the sorting out of the various empirical issues that characterize energy prices. Over time, the ability to model energy price changes will improve, but at this stage good judgment is as important as good econometrics.

NOTES TO CHAPTER 2

1. See, for example, Miller (1976), and the discussions referenced therein.
2. For a brief discussion of the reactions of various OECD countries to the rise in oil prices, see OECD (1977), pp. 68–74.
3. For theoretical work on the effects of energy price increases, see Gordon (1975a), E. Phelps (1978), and R. Solow (1980). For the effect in an open economy, see Bruno and Sachs (in press). Dohner (1978) presents an analysis similar to that of Bruno and Sachs. Relevant empirical work includes Eckstein (1978), Pierce and Enzler (1974), Mork and Hall (1980a, 1980b), Hudson and Jorgenson (1978b), and the papers in this volume.
4. A more detailed discussion of the 1973 oil embargo may be found in the papers contained in "The Oil Crisis: In Perspective," *Daedalus*, vol. 104, no. 4, Fall 1975. See also Fried and Schultze (1975). On the Iranian oil crisis, see Mancke (1980) and Verleger (1979).
5. The material in this section is drawn largely from Mancke (1980).
6. As compiled by Mancke (1980, p. 787).
7. This point is stressed by Mancke (1980).
8. Adelman (1972), Appendix V–A—especially Table V–A–4, p. 342.
9. At this time, posted prices were used for tax calculations, rather than the sale price of oil. Thus, the posted price of $11.65 in January 1974 resulted

in government receipts, or "take," of $7 per barrel. OPEC governments increased their equity shares in producing companies in the 1970s, raising their receipts as a fraction of the posted price. Thus, the increase in the price at which U.S. oil companies acquired OPEC oil was somewhat higher than indicated by the rise in posted prices.

10. *Petroleum Economist,* vol. 46, no. 10, October 1979, p. 443.

11. *The Economist* (London), June 30, 1979, p. 71.

12. See, for instance, Dornbusch and Fischer (1978), Chapters 11 and 12. For an analysis of oil price rises in this framework, see Gramlich (1979).

13. This is not strictly true, for the cost of imported materials and energy will increase in a general foreign inflation, raising the aggregate supply curve somewhat. But this effect is small relative to the shift in the demand curve, which is analyzed in the text.

14. A note on measurement. GNP is measured net of imports, and so measured real GNP and domestic income would both be reduced at any level of goods and services production. Figures 2–2 and 2–3 show the volume of goods production, not GNP.

15. Here, as elsewhere in this paper, the relative price of energy in the United States is measured by the ratio of the wholesale price index for fuels, power, and related products to the GNP deflator.

16. For a constant elasticity of substitution (CES) production function in energy and other inputs, the first-order condition is:

$$P_E \;=\; a \left(\frac{Y}{E}\right)^{\frac{1}{\sigma}},$$

where Y is output, E is energy, P_E its relative price, and σ the elasticity of substitution. Taking logs gives the results in the text.

17. C. Phelps and Smith (1977) have argued that petroleum price controls were unsuccessful in holding down petroleum product prices, and that lower domestic crude oil costs were reflected in higher refinery margins. This is difficult to believe for a number of reasons. First, it would have been illegal, and the Refinery Audit Program has resulted in penalties to several petroleum companies. Second, the rise in U.S. gasoline prices in early 1980 at a time when spot prices were falling and the fact that the U.S. petrochemical industry ran at full capacity when there was substantial slack in Europe, are inconsistent with the thesis.

18. Precisely, this is true if the price elasticity of demand for energy is less than unity.

19. Berndt and Wood (1975, 1979) find complementarity, whereas Griffin and Gregory (1976) find substitutability. Other econometric studies have split on this issue, with cross-sectional studies tending to indicate substitutability. The finding of substitutability in cross-sectional work is consistent with the argument advanced in the text.

20. See, for instance, Hausman (1979), Hirst and Carney (1979), and Darmstadter et al. (1977).

21. This assumes that the future relative price of energy is known with reasonable certainty. If the future relative price of energy is uncertain (has a high variance), investors may be unwilling to commit themselves to a design choice appropriate to a particular relative price. The investment (or lack thereof) of U.S. auto firms in small-car capacity after the 1974 rise in oil prices may be symptomatic of this effect.

22. Nominal expenditure converted to 1972 dollars using the nonresidential fixed investment deflator. Both series are from U.S. Dept. of Commerce *1977 Business Statistics*, pp. 5, 12. The increase in petroleum investment is partially offset by a fall in investment of electric utilities. The sum of the two is roughly constant in real terms from 1973 to 1976.

23. GATT, *International Trade 1974/75*, p. 3.

24. GATT, *International Trade 1975/76*, p. 5.

25. For further discussion of this point, see Salant (1978).

26. *Economic Report of the President 1975*, pp. 61–62.

27. See, for instance, Nordhaus (1972) and Godley and Nordhaus (1972). But see also Gordon (1975b) for a discussion of excess demand effects upon prices.

28. The 68 percent rise in the price of energy relative to labor is found by dividing the wholesale price index for fuels and power by the Bureau of Labor Statistics index of adjusted hourly earnings in private, nonagricultural employment (*Economic Report of the President 1980*, Tables B–56 and B–35). In a Cobb–Douglas production function with a constant capital stock, the change in labor demand is the energy share times the percentage change in the price of energy relative to labor, divided by the sum of the energy and labor shares.

29. $(0.65)(0.05) \log (1.68) = 0.0169$.

30. Gordon (1975b) has estimated the rise in the deflator for final sales (a close relative of the GNP deflator) with the cost-push effects of the energy price rises netted out. Energy prices were not the only commodity prices to rise in relative terms between 1973 and 1975; agricultural prices and raw materials prices also increased significantly. Cagan (1980) estimates that rises in prices of world traded inputs were responsible for 19.8 percentage points (about half) of the 41 percent rise in world manufactured goods prices between 1972 and 1975.

31. The index used in Figure 2–4 may overstate this effect somewhat, since it reflects prices of delivered energy and thus includes some labor and capital cost.

32. This is the time to raise the bugaboo of "validation" by the monetary authority. Of course the paths of output and of prices will depend upon the monetary policy undertaken. But to label "nonvalidation" as a neutral action, and validation a step or, in particular, a succumbing to weakness,

strikes me as misplaced. Monetary authorities do not have that much independence (or even that much single-mindedness), and one might just as easily start with validation of the price rises by increasing the money supply, and talk about possibilities of leaning against the wind.

33. Braun (1976, p. 238). Braun also argues that indexation schemes are designed to protect the lowest paid worker and therefore have a heavy weighting on foodstuffs and other commodities, making indexation schemes respond strongly to commodity price increases (p. 246).

34. See, in particular, Sachs (1979), Table 5, p. 284.

35. See, for example, McNees (1976, 1979).

36. The five forecasts he surveys are made by the Bureau of Economic Analysis of the Department of Commerce, Chase Econometrics, Data Resources Incorporated, Wharton Econometrics, and the median American Statistical Association-National Bureau of Economic Research Survey.

37. The figures for total import and nonfuel import prices are from Berner et al. (1975), Table 1, p. 15. Fuel and nonfuel imports are weighted by their value shares in the first quarter of 1973 (10.2 and 89.8 percent, respectively).

38. See Bullard (1978).

3 MACROECONOMIC ANALYSIS OF ENERGY PRICE SHOCKS AND OFFSETTING POLICIES
An Integrated Approach

Knut Anton Mork
Robert E. Hall*

I. INTRODUCTION

Energy price shocks have two kinds of economic effects. One kind has to do with energy substitution and may be referred to as aggregate supply effects. These effects include substitution in production and consumption as well as contraction of the potential output of the economy. The other kind concerns the effects on aggregate demand during the period of adjustment to a new regime of higher energy prices. Since wages do not adjust instantaneously to changes in the economic environment, the adjustment process will usually involve a period of increased inflation and unemployment, with aggregate output falling short of its long-run potential.

In our view, these two types of effects are equally important, and both should be considered in a successful analysis of energy price shocks. Yet, in the numerous attempts to analyze the macroeconomic effects of the 1973–1974 oil price increase,[1] there has been a tendency to study in isolation only one of the two aspects while ignoring the other. For example, Hudson and Jorgenson (1978b),

*Research Associate, M.I.T. Energy Laboratory, and Professor of Economics and Senior Fellow, Department of Economics and The Hoover Institution, Stanford University, respectively. Financial support from the National Science Foundation under grant no. 7910364–DAR, and from the M.I.T. Center for Energy Policy Research, is gratefully acknowledged. The authors are, of course, solely responsible for errors and shortcomings.

43

using a long-term interindustry growth model, and Eckstein (1978), using a short-run macroeconomic model, give very different accounts of what happened to the U.S. economy during the mid-1970s.

Our own modeling effort represents a serious attempt to integrate the analysis of the two kinds of effects. Our main objective has been to present a coherent explanation of the principal forces at work; on the other hand, we have been less concerned with detail than many other authors. In the interest of clarity, our model has been kept deliberately on a relatively modest scale, consisting of about ten basic equations. Although interesting and important aspects of the economy are necessarily overlooked this way, this framework has proved rich enough to allow, for example, a comprehensive quantitative study of the role of energy in the 1974–1975 experience of inflation and recession.[2]

The model assumes that goods and services are produced by labor, capital, and energy. The demand for inputs to production is modeled according to the modern theory of production. The macroeconomic structure of our model includes a financial system, which enables us to study various aspects of inflation and monetary policy. The model incorporates the hypothesis of rational expectations, but it is also somewhat Keynesian in treating money wages as predetermined in the short run. In our model, wages respond slowly to unexpected changes in energy prices (and to all other surprises in the economy). During the period following an energy price increase but before the accommodating change in the wage, labor is priced too high for full employment. Furthermore, the price level increases because wages fail to decline to offset the increase in energy prices. Our model deals explicitly with the forces of aggregate demand that produce this unhappy combination of high inflation and high unemployment. At the same time, it also deals with the problems of factor substitution and the effects on long-run supply. The contraction of potential output adds to the short-run problems caused by the effects on aggregate demand, and changes in factor intensities affect employment and investment demand.

When energy is partly imported, as in the United States of the 1970s, another consideration links output and employment to an unexpected increase in energy prices—higher prices make the United States poorer and so reduce the level of consumption in real terms. Often this is compared to the imposition of a tax on U.S. consumers, with the proceeds going to foreigners. Oil exporters acquire claims upon the United States and face the choice of accumulating the claims or cashing them in for goods produced in the United States. Our model does not attempt to explain the choices of oil producers in this regard, but uses a guess that they spend a relatively small fraction of their new income on U.S. goods. This seems consistent with observations on actual behavior in recent years.

This chapter is organized as follows. Section II introduces our model. Section III presents the results of an effort to apply the model to an analysis of the 1979 energy price shock, whereas offsetting policies are discussed in Section IV. Section V offers some conclusions.

II. THE MODEL

Our model was constructed on the basis of the one used by Hall (1978a), but contains some important extensions and revisions.[3] The present model treats the economy as having two sectors, goods and energy. Energy is viewed as primary energy, such as crude oil, natural gas at the wellhead, and coal at the minemouth. For simplicity, there is a single price of energy, though it should be recognized that this is only a rough approximation of reality.

Only the goods sector is fully represented in the model. It combines labor, capital, and energy to produce goods. The term "goods" covers all types of goods and services and includes finished energy products such as gasoline and electricity. Total goods production is allocated among consumption, investment in the goods sector, government expenditures, net export of goods, and deliveries to the energy sector. It differs from real Gross National Product (GNP) by the amount of the last item, which is small, and net energy imports.

The Basic Model Without Rigidities

The model of the goods-producing sector is built around the skeleton of a neoclassical growth model. In the absence of wage and price rigidities and of lags in the investment process, it is very simply described. It has a capital accumulation equation:

$$K_t = I_t + (1 - \delta)K_{t-1} , \tag{1}$$

where K_t is the stock of capital at time t, I_t is investment in period t, and δ is the (constant) rate of depreciation. The production possibility constraint is represented in dual form as the unit cost function:

$$\phi(e^{-\mu_1 t} w_t, P_{Kt}, P_{Et}) \ , \qquad (2)$$

where w_t is the wage rate, P_{Kt} the nominal rental price of capital, and P_{Et} the price of energy. Labor-specific technical progress is assumed, with a constant exponential rate μ_1. In the absence of an investment lag, unit cost equals marginal cost. Thus, assuming profit maximization and competitive markets, this simplified version of the model equates P, the money price of goods, to unit cost as defined in (2).

The demand for labor is derived from (2) by Shephard's lemma as:

$$L_t = e^{-\mu_1 t} \phi_L (e^{-\mu_1 t} w_t, P_{Kt}, P_{Et}) Y_t \ , \qquad (3)$$

where L_t is the level of employment, Y_t gross output from the goods sector, and ϕ_L the partial derivative of ϕ with respect to its first argument. Demand functions for capital and energy are derived analogously as:

$$K_t = \phi_K (e^{-\mu_1 t} w_t, P_{Kt}, P_{Et}) Y_t \ , \qquad (4)$$

$$E_t = \phi_E (e^{-\mu_1 t} w_t, P_{Kt}, P_{Et}) Y_t \ . \qquad (5)$$

The supply of capital is given by (1) as the result of current and past savings, the supply of labor is assumed exogenous, and energy is assumed to be supplied perfectly elastically at the exogenously given price.

The cost function (2) is specified as a flexible (in this case, translog) functional form. Its properties can be described in terms of its demand and substitution elasticities. In our model, the own price elasticity of energy demand is about -0.3, and the partial elasticities of substitution are about zero for capital and energy, and unity for capital and labor. Since the unit cost function is homogeneous of degree one, all the other demand and substitution elasticities can be derived from these three elasticities. The low own elasticity for energy is reasonable, since our definition of energy includes primary energy only. It is also supported by empirical evidence by Mork (1978a). Berndt (1976) and many others have found strong evidence for the unitary elasticity of substitution between capital and labor.

The sign and magnitude of the elasticity of substitution between capital and energy is the subject of a current controversy.[4] We expect to return to a discussion of this elasticity and its significance at a later stage. Our choice of a zero elasticity is supported by the evidence of Hudson and Jorgenson (1978b), who find a near-zero net change in aggregate capital intensity as a result of the 1973−1974 energy price increase.

Consumer behavior in our model is formulated on the basis of the life cycle–permanent income hypothesis. As shown by Hall (1978b), this hypothesis implies that the time series behavior of consumption can be approximated as a random walk with a trend. Since our model is nonstochastic, we translate this into an exponential consumption path–consumers always plan a constant growth of consumption. However, when new information arrives, such as a change in the price of energy, they make an immediate once-and-for-all adjustment to the level of consumption. This yields the formulation:

$$C_t = C_o e^{gt} , \tag{6}$$

where C_t is aggregate consumption, and C_o is chosen so that the resulting consumption path is the highest attainable, given current and expected future income. We assume that consumption is unaffected by real interest rates, in the sense that the rate of growth of planned consumption does not depend on the real interest rate.

The real part of the model is closed by the identity describing the distribution of gross output:

$$Y_t = C_t + I_t + X_t + G_t , \tag{7}$$

where X_t and G_t are net exports of (nonenergy) goods and governmental purchases, respectively, both of which are exogenous to the model.

The nominal price level is determined by adding the money demand equation:

$$ln(P_t Y_t / M_t) = \psi_0 + \psi_1 r_t + \mu_2 t , \tag{8}$$

where M_t is the money supply (assumed exogenous), and r_t is the nominal interest rate. We use the value of gross output as our measure of the dollar volume of transactions. The use of nominal GNP for this purpose is one of the many reasons why macroeconomic models in existence in 1973 were unable to deal effectively with the energy price shock (see the remarks by Pierce and Enzler [1974], p. 16)—nominal GNP subtracts imports and so cancels out much of the effect of higher energy prices.

We assume the demand for money to be unit-elastic in nominal transactions with an interest elasticity around 0.2. The latter is consistent with the evidence by Goldfeld (1973, 1976). The time trend is discussed by Hall (1977).

The money demand equation is supplemented by an arbitrage condition equating the real return to money and capital:

$$r_t = P_{Kt}/P_t - \delta - \theta + (P_{t+1} - P_t)/P_t , \qquad (9)$$

where θ is the effective tax rate on the use of capital.

Short-Run Rigidities

The formulation presented above is suitable for modeling the long-term, or supply-side, effects of energy price shocks. Integration of the short-run aggregate demand effects requires some important amendments reflecting wage and price rigidities and the investment lag. These amendments are described next.

The model assumes that part of investment is committed already at the time of a shock and cannot be adjusted in response to new information. This is modeled by treating capital as an aggregate of categories distinguished by lead times. A simple Cobb–Douglas specification is used for the aggregation:

$$K = K_1^{1/m} \ldots K_m^{1/m} . \qquad (10)$$

(The time subscript is omitted here and in the following equations.) In the year of an energy shock, investment in all but one category is committed already, whereas investment in the remaining category is derived from the demand for capital in analogy to (4). The following year, another category becomes "flexible," until all capital and investment is determined by present and future prices and demand. By the symmetry of (10), the levels planned before the shock will be the same—denoted $\bar{K}$—for all categories. Similarly, those categories whose levels are determined after the shock have the same level $\hat{K}$.

Thus, aggregate capital in any given year is given as:

$$K = \hat{K}^b \; \bar{K}^{1-b} \; , \tag{11}$$

where b is the fraction of capital determined after the shock. Investment in each category is derived as the amount required to yield the capital levels $\bar{K}$ or $\hat{K}$, respectively, according to (1); and aggregate investment is the sum of investment in each category. This formulation, which is adapted from Hall (1978a), does justice to the physical lags in the investment process without introducing arbitrary lags for expectation formation.

Wage rigidity is modeled analogously, except that here the wage rate, rather than the level of employment, is committed in advance, as in formal labor contracts. A constant fraction of the labor force is assumed to renegotiate wages each year. Based on current information about future demand for labor, wages are set so as to clear the labor market in expectation. When surprises happen, the committed wage rate may not clear the market, so unemployment may occur. In the years following the shock, wages are renegotiated gradually, so the labor market returns gradually to equilibrium. We summarize this hypothesis in the equation:

$$w = \hat{w}^f \; \bar{w}^{1-f} \; , \tag{12}$$

where f is the fraction of the labor market whose wages are renegotiated after the shock. The demand for labor is determined by (3), and unemployment occurs if the average wage rate exceeds the market-clearing wage $\hat{w}$.

This formulation, set forth by Hall (1978a), has been extended in our model to reflect cost-of-living wage increases and cyclical variations in labor productivity. It implies a kind of Phillips curve for the economy. However, in place of the expected inflation term, which has been the source of so much instability and conceptual ambiguity in the literature on the Phillips curve, expectations are formed using the model itself.

Our model also assumes some rigidity in the pricing of final goods and services. This is based on the common empirical finding that fluctuations in demand have little or no effect on the price level apart from the effect via wages. Also, transitory fluctuations in interest rates do not seem to affect prices appreciably. For this reason, we replace the marginal-cost-pricing assumption discussed above by an assumption of standard unit cost pricing. Whereas standard unit cost by definition is unaffected by transitory fluctuations in demand and interest rates, the cost concept as defined by (2) is affected by these forces. This can be seen from the following argument. When part of capital is committed in advance, the price of aggregate capital—which appears in (2)—can be written as:

$$P_K = \hat{P}_K^b \, \overline{P}_K^{1-b} \, , \tag{13}$$

where $\hat{P}_K$ is the market price of "flexible" capital, $\overline{P}_K$ the shadow price of committed capital, and b is as defined in (11). Interest rate fluctuations affect $\hat{P}_K$, and variations in $\overline{P}_K$ reflect short-run fluctuations in demand pressure.

Consequently, we reformulate the price equation as:

$$P = \phi(e^{-\mu_1 t} w, \, P\overline{v}, \, P_E) \, . \tag{14}$$

We use the same unit cost function as in (2), but the argument P_K is replaced by $P\overline{v}$, where $\overline{v}$ denotes a standard or normal return to capital. We define $\overline{v}$ as a weighted average of past and projected future real rental prices of capital, with the weight of past rental prices declining over time. This measure is not influenced by short-run fluctuations in output and interest rates. Furthermore, the specification (14) gives a sensible estimate of the partial impact on the price level of an energy price increase, namely the share of energy in variable cost. This is supported by empirical evidence in Mork (1978b).

Our model is compatible with the hypothesis that inflation is determined by money supply in the long run. In the short run, however, wage and price rigidity may allow substantial deviations from this rule.

III. THE 1979 ENERGY PRICE SHOCK

We have recently published a paper that reports the results of an analysis of the macroeconomic effects of the sudden increase in the world price of oil that followed the Iranian revolution.[5] The analysis, which used the model outlined above, was carried out in the summer of 1979, so the large increases in the price of crude oil that took place in the second half of the year are not reflected in the analysis.

We assumed an increase in the world price of crude oil from $12.70 in 1978 to $21.50 in the second quarter of 1979. The latter price was assumed to prevail throughout 1979, to increase to $24.50 in 1980, and to stay constant in real terms thereafter. As for the prices of domestic fuels, we assumed percentage increases by the same amounts for domestic crude oil,[6] and by half as much for coal and natural gas. However, because of long-term contracts and regulations of utilities and other energy markets, we assumed a passthrough of only 80 percent of primary energy prices to the final consumer in 1979. For 1980 and beyond, the passthrough was assumed to be complete. Of the total price increase, we assumed that 9 percentage points per year could be attributed to the expected effect of overall inflation and treated the rest as unanticipated increases.

The results of our analysis, which are summarized in Table 3−1, indicate a serious dislocation of the U.S. economy because of this shock. The effects on inflation are projected to be most serious in the first year, with almost 2 percentage points added to the inflation rate. The real effects are equally serious, but occur with a short lag. The shortfall in real output is projected as $15 billion (1972) or 1 percent in 1979, and $55 billion or almost 4 percent in 1980. The fluctuation is largest for investment activity, which is projected to

Table 3−1.   Summary of projected effects of energy shock.

	1979	1980	1981
Extra inflation (percentage points per year)	1.8	1.3	0.1
Extra growth in real GNP (percentage points per year)	−1.1	−2.8	0.4
Extra investment (percentage of level in absence of shock)	3.6	−12.6	−14.8
Extra consumption (percentage of level in absence of shock)	−2.6	−2.9	−2.3
Extra unemployment (percentage points)	0.4	1.2	0.9

reach a bottom level in 1981 with a shortfall of $34 billion. Consumption is projected to decrease by 2.5 to 3 percent.[7] Government expenditure was assumed to follow its past trend in real terms, whereas net export of nonenergy goods was expected to rise by $3 billion (1972). We assumed, however, that this increase would not take effect until 1981, as the recession was expected to slow down export demand from other countries. Unemployment is projected to increase, but with a short lag, like real output. The largest increase, a little more than 1 percentage point, is projected for 1980.

These effects can be interpreted in terms of the two kinds of effects referred to in the introduction to this chapter. Consumption is affected on both accounts. First, the higher price of energy reduces the long-run supply of goods as a result of substitution away from energy. Second, the energy price increase reduces the demand for labor in general equilibrium, so the market-clearing wage falls. However, since wages are rigid, this decline fails to materialize in the short run, so employment falls temporarily. As a result, production falls below the new long-term growth path of the economy. This temporary shortfall, like the permanent downward shift in the economy's supply schedule, represents a real loss of income, so consumption declines. Domestic consumers are also worse off because of the substantial transfer of income to oil-rich nations, although this is mitigated somewhat by the fact that some of this transfer is accumulated in the form of claims on the U.S. economy. As energy exporters spend part of their new wealth on U.S. goods, export demand increases a little, but by much less than the total decline in domestic consumption.

The effect on investment falls primarily into the category of aggregate demand effects. As aggregate production falls below its long-run potential and consumption is determined by permanent income, investment must fall temporarily. From a partial point of view, this may be seen as the direct result of an interaction between financial and real forces. With money supply unchanged in nominal terms, the induced increase in the price level reduces the real supply of money. This reduction would normally drive up interest rates and thus discourage investment. However, because of the interactions with the real sector, the general equilibrium effect on the interest rate is ambiguous in our model. Investment declines nevertheless because of a strong output effect. Furthermore, in a somewhat indirect sense, the decline in investment is indeed the result of an interaction between real and financial forces, because wages are rigid in nominal terms. The assumption that money demand depends on nominal gross output, rather than nominal GNP, as the transactions variable, strengthens this effect in the model.

At the time of final editing, the U.S. economy seems to have entered an even sharper recession than the one projected in our analysis. The continued increase in the world price of oil in the second half of 1979 has probably contributed to this.[8] It appears doubtful, however, that the recession of 1980 can be blamed on energy alone, since other contractionary forces, such as the monetary tightening during the fall of 1979 and winter of 1979–80, have obviously been present as well.

IV. MACROECONOMIC POLICY RESPONSES TO THE 1979 ENERGY PRICE SHOCK

The long-run effects of higher energy prices on aggregate supply are largely unavoidable and can be alleviated by a clever choice of policy only to a limited extent. However, as we have seen, an energy shock also works on aggregate demand and pushes employment below its full-employment level. These shorter run, business-cycle responses are economically inefficient—they involve underutilization of the productive capacity of the economy. It seems likely that at least some of these effects can be offset by proper choice of economic policy. However, the problem of selecting the best policy response seems yet unresolved. A whole range of measures has been discussed in the public debate, including policies as different as synthetic fuel programs and monetary contraction. This section reviews macroeconomic policy responses to the oil price shock. Policies operating directly on energy supply or demand, important as they are, will not be discussed here.

Our model permits computation of numerical estimates of the effects of policy measures on key macroeconomic variables, including inflation, real economic growth, and employment. The policies studied are monetary expansion and contraction, fiscal expenditure policy, investment stimulus via changes in the corporate income tax, and a payroll tax cut. Personal income tax cuts are discussed as well, although some fundamental difficulties are involved in studying this policy. The policies are discussed in the context of the 1979 price shock, as projected in Section III, but the analysis applies to energy price shocks in general.

Our analysis suggests that attempts to offset the energy-induced inflation by contractionary monetary policy may have severe consequences for employment and economic growth. Monetary expansion is preferred to increases in public spending because of the negative side effects of the latter on inflation and capital formation. As a pro-investment policy, an increase in the investment tax credit seems attractive and is not found to be very inflationary. A payroll tax cut seems a possibility for cutting inflation in the short run and aiding employment and economic growth at the same time.

Monetary and Fiscal Expenditure Policy

Macroeconomic policies to offset energy price shocks face two important conflicts. The first is the dilemma of inflation against employment. The recent history of severe inflation in the United States has made national economic policy as concerned about offsetting the inflationary impact of an energy price shock as in shoring up employment and output. A policy to limit inflation—specifically, through monetary contraction—could worsen the adverse effects of the energy shock on real economic activity. Fiscal expansion to maintain employment and output might push inflation even beyond the current high levels attributable to the direct effects of the energy shock. Our analysis suggests a way out of this dilemma, however, as it traces the indirect effects of alternative policies through capital formation. Policies with favorable effects on investment have a significant advantage because they cushion the real shock without too high a price in added inflation. A limited monetary accommodation of the energy shock is attractive for this reason. The opposite response— monetary contraction—is the only effective instrument for restraining inflation in the long run, but is unsuitable as a response to an energy shock because it works with a long lag and has a depressing effect on investment in the short run. Similarly, we find that fiscal stimulus, through income tax cuts or increases in government expenditures, is even less suitable because of its unfavorable effect on investment. Furthermore, we find that a sufficiently expansionary fiscal policy to offset the employment effects of the new energy shock would bring about unacceptable rates of inflation.

The other problem is the issue of timing. For accommodative monetary policy, we find it essential that the monetary authority act quickly to expand money supply immediately after the shock. Usually this means that monetary action is needed several months before the economy reaches the bottom of the recession. A belated monetary response will have to be that much stronger and runs a larger risk of overheating the economy.

For fiscal policy, the main timing problem comes from the long decision process. We find that fiscal action is much more powerful when the government makes swift, surprising moves. Thus, although a public policy debate is necessary in a democratic system, a dragged-out discussion about details of a policy package is likely to weaken its impact substantially. We consider this a major weakness of fiscal policy.

Table 3-2 shows a summary of the estimated effects of alternative monetary and fiscal policies as they would have been if introduced immediately after the 1979 energy price shock. For the sake of comparison, the two policies are assumed to operate at levels sufficient to stabilize unemployment at around 6 percent. The monetary expansion is assumed to take the form of increasing monetary growth from 5 to 6 percent in 1979, from 6 to 8 percent in 1980, and from 6 to 7 percent thereafter. For fiscal expenditure policy, we study the effect of an exogenous increase in spending of $23 billion (1972) in 1979, $96 billion in 1980, and $100 billion in 1981. Obviously, these are far in excess of any likely fiscal response, but they are the magnitudes required to stabilize employment in our model.

Fiscal expenditure policy would have been by far the more inflationary alternative, increasing the inflation rate by 1 percentage point in 1979 and 2 percentage points in 1980. Furthermore, although it stabilizes employment, it has a severe negative impact on economic growth. Of course, our projections overstate the likely inflationary and antigrowth effects of expenditure policy because we study an expenditure response that is far larger than any remotely likely to be entertained by national economic policymakers.

Our results are much more favorable for a monetary response to the employment effects of the energy shock. The magnitude of the necessary response is quite small if done in time—1 percent extra monetary growth in 1979, 2 percent extra in 1980, and 1 percent extra in later years. Monetary stimulus achieves most of its effects by raising investment; the resulting additional capital formation enlarges

Table 3–2. Estimates of what the effects of monetary and fiscal policies to stabilize employment would have been if introduced in early 1979.

	1979	1980	1981
Monetary response			
Extra inflation (percentage points per year)	−0.7	−0.2	0.4
Extra real GNP growth (percentage points per year)	1.6	2.3	1.1
Extra money growth (percentage points per year)	1.0	2.0	1.0
Fiscal response			
Extra inflation (percentage points per year)	0.9	2.0	1.7
Extra real GNP growth (percentage points per year)	1.7	1.1	−2.7
Extra government expenditure required ($bill 1972)	23.0	96.0	100.0

the productive capacity of the economy and moderates the effect on inflation. Ultimately, higher money growth means higher inflation, but in the first few years after the energy shock and monetary offset, the favorable effect on capital formation and the unresponsiveness of wages assumed in our analysis combine to hold total inflation to a reasonable level.

The actual conduct of monetary and fiscal policy did not follow any of these paths in 1979. Rather, monetary policy was accommodative early in the year, and turned later toward lower money growth. A tax cut for 1980 was discussed seriously but never actually introduced. We have serious misgivings about the Federal Reserve Board's tightening of money supply in late 1979 and early 1980.

Though moderation of monetary growth is a necessity over the next several years in order to slow down inflation, the sudden, sharply contractionary move at that time was unwise in our view. It suggests a neglect of the central goals of maintaining capital formation and real growth.

Estimated effects of fiscal and monetary policy alternatives for 1980 are listed in Table 3−3.[9] The necessary increase in money growth to stabilize employment in 1980 is much larger than what would have been needed if action had been taken immediately.

Table 3−3. Estimates of the likely effects of monetary and fiscal policies to stabilize employment if introduced in 1980.

	1980	1981	1982
Monetary response			
Extra inflation (percentage points per year)	−1.2	−0.6	0.8
Extra real GNP growth (percentage points per year)	1.4	3.5	2.4
Extra money growth (percentage points per year)	3.0	2.0	2.0
Unanticipated fiscal response			
Extra inflation (percentage points per year)	0.9	1.0	−0.0
Extra real GNP growth (percentage points per year)	4.4	−1.8	−2.1
Extra government expenditure required ($bill 1972)	71.0	70.0	0.0
Anticipated fiscal response			
Extra inflation (percentage points per year)	2.3	1.7	−0.0
Extra real GNP growth (percentage points per year)	−1.7	−3.0	−2.0
Extra government expenditure required ($bill 1972)	116.0	100.0	0.0

Again, the favorable effect on capital formation holds inflation to a reasonable level in the first few years. We anticipate, however, that the jump in money growth needed in 1980 would create expectations of increased future growth rates of the money supply, so in the long run this policy might increase inflation by a couple of percentage points.

The effects of a fiscal expenditure policy depend crucially on whether or not the economy already expects such a program. If it does (one year in advance), the necessary outlay for stabilizing employment is about one and one-half times larger. The effects on inflation and economic growth are also much less favorable in this case. And even if the fiscal stimulus comes as a surprise, it is more inflationary than monetary policy and is much more harmful to capital formation and economic growth.

Rather than rely entirely on raising government expenditures, actual policy is likely to try to stimulate private consumption expenditures by temporarily cutting personal income taxes. The economic impacts of a successful policy to raise consumption would be very similar to those of an increase in government expenditure—in particular, part of the increase would come at the expense of capital formation and subsequent real growth. However, we do not pursue the analysis of a personal tax cut because we, like many other economists, are skeptical of the ability of a temporary tax cut to stimulate consumption in any substantial way. In our analysis, if fiscal policy is to offset the adverse effects of the energy shock on real output, it will have to rely mainly on very large increases in government expenditures, with highly unfavorable side effects on growth and inflation.

Tax Cuts for Inputs to Production

Fiscal expenditure and income tax cuts are only two of many possible options for the makers of fiscal policy. Two other types of stimulus to the economy are currently under consideration, namely, encouraging investment by changing the rules of corporate taxation and encouraging employment by cutting payroll taxes. Our results for such policies are quite favorable. Both policies stimulate investment, as does monetary expansion, but their long-run effects are less adverse than for the latter. Also, they contribute less to the federal deficit than would a fiscal expenditure policy.

The estimated effects of changes in the investment tax credit for 1980 and 1981 are summarized in Table 3-4. The tax credit is taken at a level sufficient to stabilize employment at around 6 percent in 1980 and 1981, so the results are comparable to those of monetary and fiscal expenditure policy. The policy is assumed to have been announced—and to take effect as well—at the beginning of 1980. The moderate increase in inflation for the first two years contrasts sharply with fiscal expenditure policy. The reduction in inflation in the third year accompanies the decline in real growth as policy returns to normal in 1982. This decline in growth could be avoided by making the increased credit permanent or by a smoother return to normal. The effect on long-run growth (after ten years in our model) is, however, positive, whereas fiscal expenditure policy lowers the long-term growth path of the economy. The revenue loss for the investment tax credit seems well within the limits of realistic policy-making.

Table 3-5 shows the estimated outcome of a cut in payroll taxes. Our model hypothesizes that much of the economic dislocation of an energy price increase is attributable to the unresponsiveness of wages. When energy prices rise, either the overall price level must rise or wage costs must fall. A cut in payroll taxes makes it possible for employers' wage costs to fall without a corresponding decline in wages received by workers. We find that a cut of 4.5 percentage points

Table 3-4. Estimated effects of a fiscal policy aimed specifically at stimulating investment: temporary increase in the investment tax credit.

	1980	1981	1982
Extra inflation (percentage points per year)	0.2	0.1	-2.5
Extra real GNP growth (percentage points per year)	3.8	-0.0	-4.5
Increase in investment tax credit (percentage points)	6.9	4.9	0.0
Revenue loss ($bill 1972)	18.5	14.0	0.4

Table 3-5.   Estimated effects of payroll tax cut.

	1980	1981	1982
Extra inflation (percentage points per year)	−6.0	1.4	2.1
Extra real GNP growth (percentage points per year)	3.9	−0.1	−4.2
Reduction in payroll tax rate (percentage points)	4.5	3.2	0.0
Revenue loss ($bill 1972)	44.3	26.0	2.0

in payroll taxes in 1980 and 3.2 percentage points in 1981 would largely eliminate the impact of the energy price shock on employment. Inflation in 1980 would be as much as 6 percentage points lower with this cut than in the case of no policy response. Because the policy would concentrate all of its effect of lowering costs in 1980, it would increase inflation somewhat in 1981, and, in 1982, when payroll taxes returned to their original level, inflation would be about 2 percentage points worse than in the base case. The net effect on the price level through 1982 would be favorable because the policy would stimulate capital formation.[10] The extremely favorable effect on inflation in 1980 depends on a direct linkage between prices and labor costs, which is assumed in our analysis and in most other macroeconomic models. This point may be worth further investigation, but the results so far seem very promising for this kind of policy. It is somewhat more expensive than a direct investment stimulus, but is substantially cheaper than fiscal expenditure policy, and promises a far more favorable effect on inflation than either of these. Perhaps this is the right time to try an experiment along these lines.

V. CONCLUDING REMARKS

Our model of the U.S. economy suggests that it is vulnerable in important ways to unexpected increases in the world oil price. An oil shock drives down investment and pushes employment below its full-employment level. In addition, U.S. consumers suffer a loss in real income, which makes them reduce consumption.

The latter response is inescapable and would occur even in an economy that was able to respond to the oil shock in a fully efficient way. The short-run underutilization of the productive capacity of the economy can, however, be mitigated by macroeconomic policy. Our review of the options open to policymakers has called attention to the role of capital formation in the alternative effects of different policies. Some policies may be classified as proinvestment: monetary accommodation, investment tax credit, and payroll tax cut. Because they favor capital formation, they help offset inflation. Other policies are antiinvestment: monetary tightness and increases in federal spending. Unfortunately, the present movements of macroeconomic policy seem to be in exactly this second direction. We favor as an alternative the following combination: monetary policy aiming to achieve growth rates of monetary aggregates at approximately their averages over the past five years, without any sudden reduction in growth but with a commitment to gradual reductions in money growth over the forthcoming five years. Second, a temporary increase in the investment tax credit of 2 or 3 percentage points. Third, a permanent reduction in payroll taxes of several percentage points (with the necessary revenue for financing Social Security benefits coming from general federal revenues). This package would help put the United States back on the path of higher capital accumulation and growth, from which it was deflected by the first energy shock in 1974 and from which a further deflection is threatening.

NOTES TO CHAPTER 3

1. An excellent survey of this literature is presented by Robert S. Dohner in the preceding chapter.
2. See Mork and Hall (1980b).
3. A more complete presentation, with an application to the 1974–1975 recession, can be found in Mork and Hall (1980b).
4. A discussion of the empirical evidence is found in Berndt and Wood (1975, 1979) and Griffin and Gregory (1976); whereas Hogan (1979), J. Solow (1979), and Mork (1980) discuss the conceptual issues involved.
5. Mork and Hall (1980a). The reader is referred to this paper for more detailed results.

6. This implies an assumption that the price equalization program for crude oil had no effect on petroleum product prices. This view has been advocated by C. Phelps and Smith. (1977). We recognize the arguments against this view, however, and consider it an oversimplification. On the other hand, the assumption that this program was fully effective, as used in Chapters 4 and 5 of this volume, seems to us even more extreme.

7. From formula (6) above, the reader might expect the percentage shortfall in consumption to be uniform for all years. For the actual runs of the model, however, we introduced a temporary reduction in consumption below its long-term path. This adjustment, which was done ad hoc, reflects the once-and-for-all stock adjustment for consumer durables.

8. Even though our assumptions about the price responses of domestic fuels may have been exaggerated, the actual increase in average energy prices from 1978 to early 1980 is likely to have exceeded the total increase implied by our assumptions.

9. The reader should note at this point that the consequences of the oil price increases of late 1979 are not included in this analysis.

10. In our previous paper (Mork and Hall 1980a), we reported somewhat different results for a payroll tax cut. The discrepancy is due to a difference in perspective: The policy studied in that paper was assumed to be announced in 1979 and to take effect in 1980.

4 SHOCK INFLATION, CORE INFLATION, AND ENERGY DISTURBANCES IN THE DRI MODEL

Otto Eckstein *

Energy has become a macro topic. Along with industrial capacity, energy is the effective supply constraint of the economy, is frequently a decisive factor for inflation, growth, and employment performance, and therefore resides at the very center of macro policy.

As a result, the major macroeconomic models used for forecasting and policy analysis now incorporate energy sectors, which are designed to trace the effects of energy and related supply shocks on the economy. This chapter summarizes the energy analysis embodied in the structure of the Data Resources, Inc. (DRI) Model of the U.S. Economy, an 800-equation construct used for both short- and long-term studies. Because the model is intended to represent the economic process in considerable detail, the energy sector traces through numerous micro effects.

Detail can hide as well as reveal. To provide a conceptual structure that shows the basic forces, I have recently developed a small model of core, demand, and shock inflation. It is largely recursive to the U.S. macro model and therefore benefits from the full detail. Both models are used here to analyze the impact of the two energy shocks—1973–1974 and 1979–1980—on the economy, and to examine macroeconomic policy choices for the 1980s.

*President, Data Resources, Inc., and Paul M. Warburg Professor of Economics, Harvard University.

Figure 4–1.   The energy sector of the DRI U.S. macro model: major linkages.

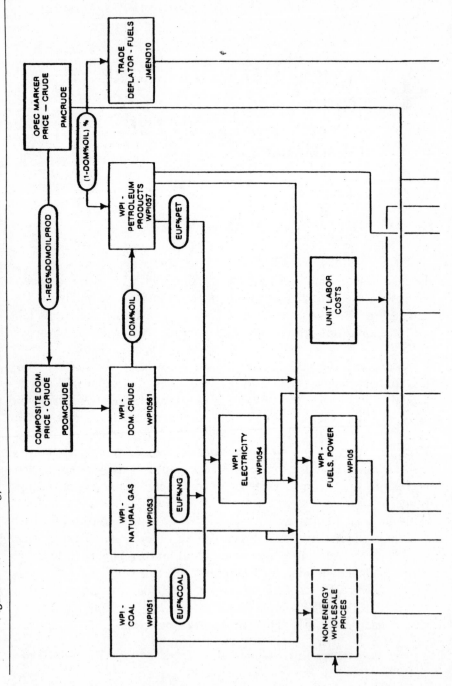

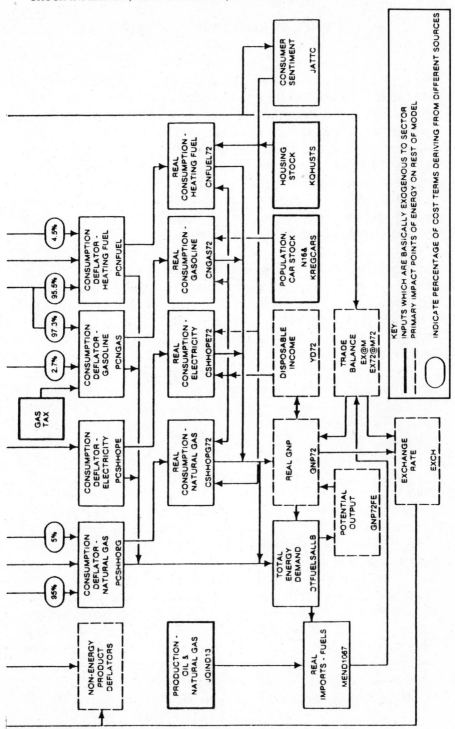

I. THE ENERGY SECTOR IN THE DRI MODEL
OF THE U.S. ECONOMY

Figure 4–1 presents the detailed structure of the energy sector in the DRI Model. The exogenous variables are an index of the OPEC marker price, production of domestic oil and natural gas, major tax rates levied by the various levels of government on gasoline, crude oil, electricity, and so forth, and the price control schedules on the various domestic energy sources.[1] In addition, the macro model treats energy supply estimates derived from solutions of DRI's energy models as exogenous, including the breakdown of electricity generation by source (coal, natural gas, and petroleum), and the domestic production of coal, natural gas, and petroleum.

On the cost side, the model traces the prices of imported and domestic oil into the retail prices of final energy products bought by consumers, such as gasoline, electricity, natural gas, and heating oil. Prices of the basic energy sources are traced through stage-of-processing equations to the various wholesale prices for different industries, and into retail prices generally.

On the demand side, the several household demands for energy are derived from consumption functions that include relative price terms, as well as the household stocks to which energy use is related, such as housing and automobiles adjusted for their efficiency ratings. Other demand is derived from more aggregative equations that include price elasticities.

On the supply side, energy is one of four factors in the model's aggregate production function, along with capital, labor, and the stock of research and development. The production function is currently of the Cobb–Douglas form, but differs somewhat from the conventional formulation. The capital stock is revalued by the inverse of its average age to reflect the effects of embodied technical change. The cyclical influence on factor use is measured by the utilization rate of manufacturing capacity and by the change in average hours worked. The deleterious effect of the tax system on productivity is measured by the average effective rate of personal and payroll taxes. Indirectly, energy also affects other supplies. Industry investment equations include the energy sector and help determine aggregate investment and the physical capital stock. The growth rate of the residential construction stock depends upon the rental price of housing, which includes energy among the operating costs. The supply of finance to the economy as a whole is affected by energy, both through the general impact of prices on the financial system and through capital requirements of the energy industries.

Energy has various other indirect effects on the economy. Consumer sentiment, one determinant of consumption, contains energy prices as a separate term, and should (but does not yet) contain a term for energy supply disruption. The exchange rate in the model is affected by the trade balance, which is, of course, heavily influenced by oil imports.

The model calculates the aggregate demand for energy in terms of quadrillion Btus (quads). In the case of household demands, the separate consumption functions are used to calculate energy requirements directly. In the case of industrial, transportation, commercial, and other demands, the equations are very simple, relying on activity levels at relative energy prices, leaving it to the DRI energy model to provide the more detailed estimates. To ensure consistency, the macro and energy models can be solved simultaneously. Thus, the total energy demand estimates of the macro model are used mainly for simulation exercises and to identify the oil import problem.

In the current version of the DRI Model, the oil import bill is calculated as a residual. Given total energy demand and exogenous domestic energy supplies, the import requirement is simply the difference. It then becomes a matter of further analysis to assess whether OPEC will, in fact, make the calculated supplies available and at what price. If supplies fall short, policy must choose among allocations, rationing, higher prices, reduced aggregate activity, or queuing, which deteriorates efficiency of resource use.

A more technical account of the energy sector in the DRI Macro Model is presented in the technical appendix[2] to this chapter.

II. THE CORE INFLATION MODEL

An aggregate conceptual framework has been developed as a near-recursive component of the DRI Model to improve understanding of the inflation process. This model distinguishes three kinds of inflation: core inflation, demand inflation, and shock inflation.

Core inflation is the trend rate of increase of the aggregate supply price of labor and capital. The core rate originates in the long-term expectations of inflation in the minds of households and businesses, in the contractual arrangements that sustain the wage-price momentum, and in the tax system. Core inflation can be increased or decreased by the particular circumstances of any short period; however, it can be modified only gradually. No short-term experience or event will undo the cumulative effects of history on expectations.

Figure 4–2 shows the core inflation rate since 1960. The core inflation rate improved early in the period and was nearly eliminated by 1964. Since then it has deteriorated steadily, even in years when the measured inflation rate showed dramatic improvement. It is now moving toward 10 percent. Figure 4–3 shows the impulses that led to this deterioration.

The conceptual structure can be outlined as follows. The total inflation rate of a period, as measured by the Consumer Price Index (CPI), is equal to the sum of the three separate inflation sources: demand, shock, and core.

$$\dot{p} = \dot{p}_c + \dot{p}_d + \dot{p}_s , \tag{1}$$

where:

$$\dot{p} = \text{inflation rate,}$$
$$\dot{p}_c = \text{core rate,}$$
$$\dot{p}_d = \text{demand rate, and}$$
$$\dot{p}_s = \text{shock rate.}$$

The core rate of inflation can be viewed as the rate that would occur on the economy's long-term growth path if the growth path were free of shocks and if the state of demand were neutral, as in long-run equilibrium. The core rate reflects those price increases made necessary by increases in the trend costs of the inputs to production. The cost increases, in turn, are largely a function of underlying price expectations. In a competitive Cobb–Douglas economy with Hicks–neutral technological change, the long-term equilibrium price, p_c, can be written as:[3]

$$p_c = Aq^{a_1} w^{a_2} e^{-bt} , \tag{2}$$

where q is the rental price of the capital required per unit of output, w is the wage rate of the unit labor requirement, b is the aggregate factor productivity rate of technological progress, and a_1 and a_2 are the Cobb–Douglas factor share weights, summing to unity.

Figure 4–2.   The core inflation rate and the consumer price index (*year-over-year percentage change*).

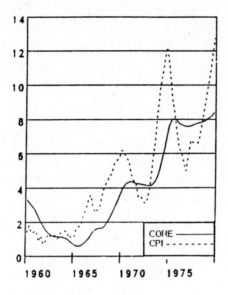

Figure 4–3.   The inflation impulse curve[a] (*percentage change*).

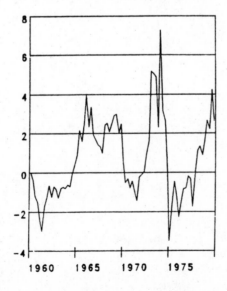

a. The sum of demand and shock impulses.

The *core inflation rate* is the change in the long-term equilibrium price along the balanced growth path. It can be written as:

$$\dot{p}_c = a_2 \dot{q} + a_2 \dot{w} - b \ . \tag{3}$$

The rental price of capital depends on the relative price of capital goods, depreciation and other tax parameters, interest rates, and equity rates of return. Let:

$$\dot{q} = \alpha(r, J_q) \ , \tag{4}$$

where r is the market cost of financial capital and J is the tax variable. Financial cost is determined by the long-term inflation expectations embodied in nominal interest rates and equity yields, so:

$$\dot{q} = \alpha(\dot{p}_q^e, J_q) \ . \tag{5}$$

Similarly, wages on the equilibrium path are determined by the price expectations underlying wage claims, and by the tax-transfer system, or are based on:

$$\dot{w} = \beta(\dot{p}_w^e, J_w) \ . \tag{6}$$

Therefore, the core rate of inflation depends on long-term price expectations in labor and capital markets, tax provisions, and factor productivity:

$$\dot{p}_c = a_1 \alpha(\dot{p}_q^e, J_q) + a_2 \beta(\dot{p}_w^e, J_w) - b. \tag{7}$$

The Core Inflation Model assumes that price expectations are formed on the basis of inflation experience, as measured by distributed lags on actual prices, and need not be the same for bond buyers as for workers. Thus:

$$\dot{p}_c = a_1 \alpha((\sum_{t=0}^{-\infty} \lambda_t \dot{p}_t), J_q) + a_2 \beta((\sum_{t=0}^{-\infty} \mu_t \dot{p}_t), J_w) - b \ , \tag{8}$$

where λ_t and μ_t are the weights attached to past inflation rates in the learning processes that form expectations.

The *demand inflation rate* will depend on utilization rates of resources. Unemployment and the operating rate of capital are both presumably pertinent, and the effects are nonlinear. Monetary and fiscal policies, foreign demands, and the dynamics of the domestic business cycle mechanism are the main forces determining demand inflation. Labor and capital supplies also affect the degree of inflationary disequilibrium created by any particular level of demand.

The *shock inflation rate* is, by definition, exogenous to the analysis. Such shocks as OPEC and food prices are in part endogenous, with aggregate demand playing the conventional price-lifting role. Here, however, they are considered to be determined primarily by noncontrollable conditions—OPEC political/economic decisions in one case, weather and crop conditions in another. Government shocks, such as payroll taxes, are considered exogenous because they are policy levers that can be controlled.

The various components of inflation must be pursued further to their root causes. The core inflation rate is partly determined by the productivity trend, which depends upon the rate of capital formation, human resource investment, energy supplies, and technological progress. The capacity utilization rate affecting demand inflation reflects supply considerations, including the tax system, as well as the level of demand created by fiscal and monetary policies and private spending propensities. A theory of investment is needed for capital supply, and a theory of labor force participation is needed for labor supply.

In effect, fully tracing the three components of inflation to root causes requires a full description of the economy such as that presented by a complete macroeconomic model. The actual implementation of the Core Inflation Model is drawn almost entirely from the 800-equation DRI Quarterly Econometric Model of the U.S. Economy. Thus, there is no need to develop a special-purpose theoretical or empirical model to conduct a full core inflation analysis, though it can be treated as a stand-alone analytical device in which its inputs— demand, shocks, the rental price of capital, the rates of wage and productivity increase—are treated as exogenous.

The large DRI Macro Model is an eclectic, detailed empirical representation of the economy. The core inflation analysis could as easily be tied into a monetarist model, in which aggregate spending is driven exclusively by the monetary factor. Apart from the particular decomposition of the problem into its three components to provide analytical focus, the core model makes strong empirical statements only in one crucial regard: The formation of price expectations for determining long-run capital and labor costs is a gradual learning process rather than a quick response to policies or other particular events. The theory is consistent with the rational expectations hypothesis in the weak sense that price expectations are free of bias when inflation proceeds around a constant trend. It is, however, inconsistent with the viewpoint that these price expectations are formed quickly from particular policies or actual price experiences.

III. ENERGY AND CORE INFLATION

Figure 4–4 shows the historical role of energy in the inflation process. Until 1973, energy had little effect on the economy's cost structure. Thereafter, the energy component of shock inflation be-

Figure 4–4. The core inflation rate (*percent*).

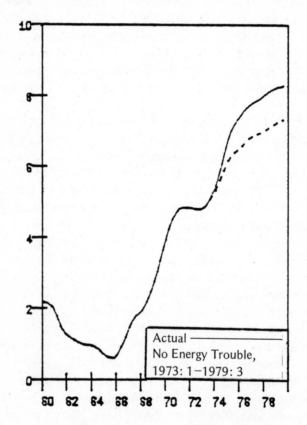

came very large. Gradually, via the expectations of workers and investors, it converted itself into core inflation. The figure shows the actual record of core inflation and contrasts it with a hypothetical path in which energy prices continue their previous moderate behavior, with annual average increases of just 5½ percent.

The comparison shows not only the importance of energy in core inflation, but also indicates that there is far more to recent inflationary experience than this one factor. The core inflation rate had risen from its brief near-zero levels of the mid–1960s to 5 percent by the time the OPEC actions began, and would have continued to worsen anyway. There were various other shocks, including food price rises, higher payroll taxes, and the decline of the dollar. Productivity faded for a variety of reasons, of which energy was only one. By the end of 1978, when the actual core inflation rate was 8.1 percent, the no-energy-trouble scenario would have placed the core rate at 7.2 percent, still a very serious figure.

IV. THE IMPACT OF ENERGY ON THE ECONOMY—A FULLER VIEW

While the core inflation analysis focuses on the fundamentals of the inflation problem, a full economic analysis, including the impact of real activity and capital formation, requires a full macro-model simulation. Tables 4–1 through 4–3 contrast a historical tracking simulation of the DRI Macro Model with a hypothetical historical solution in which energy prices rise at only a 5½ percent annual rate. The solution without the energy crisis portrays a significantly different outcome. The energy crisis was not the only factor pushing the economy off its equilibrium path in 1973–1974. However, without it, the economy would have suffered no worse than a year of a small GNP decline in 1974, and would have seen 1975 as the first year of recovery. By 1976, real GNP would have been 4 percent higher than in the historical tracking simulation.

The energy crisis was also largely responsible for the poor investment and productivity results of the last five years. In the no-energy-trouble case, investment averages 4.9 percent higher and productivity 1.7 percent higher between 1973 and 1978. This helps boost the potential output of the economy by 2 percent by 1978.

Table 4-1. Summary of tracking simulation of the U.S. economy.

	1973	1974	1975	1976	1977	1978
	Inflation Rates					
Core inflation rate	5.0	5.9	7.1	7.6	7.9	8.1
Shock inflation rate	2.9	3.9	1.1	0.6	0.8	1.1
Demand inflation rate	−1.9	1.1	1.0	−2.4	−1.8	−1.0
	Year-over-year Percentage Changes					
Real GNP	5.5	−1.4	−1.3	5.9	5.3	4.4
Total consumption	4.7	−0.9	1.8	5.9	5.0	4.5
Nonres. fixed invest.	12.3	−0.3	−13.2	5.0	8.8	8.5
Invest. in res. structures	−4.0	−24.9	−13.8	23.4	20.9	4.0
Net exports (level)	7.6	15.8	22.5	15.8	10.3	10.8
Government purchases	−0.2	2.0	1.9	0.2	2.0	1.7
Imported fuel price	44.5	242.7	11.0	7.6	7.7	2.5
Personal consumption deflator	5.5	10.9	8.1	5.1	5.7	6.8
Output per hour	1.8	−3.3	1.9	3.6	1.8	1.0
Potential GNP	4.2	3.3	3.2	2.7	2.6	3.0
	Percentage Points					
Unemployment rate	4.8	5.6	8.5	7.7	7.0	6.0

This analysis repeats the work reported in greater detail in my recent book (Eckstein 1978, Chapter 9), but performed on the current version of the DRI Model. During the last three years, the model has become considerably more elaborate by including the full energy sector, as well as various new supply formations and a heightened sensitivity of the wage-price block. Despite various changes, the results are very similar to the figures reported in the earlier book.[4]

V. EFFECTS OF THE SECOND OPEC SHOCK

In January 1979, the industrial world experienced the second OPEC shock. As Table 4-4 shows, the total magnitudes of the current round are very similar to the 1974 experience. These figures and the following analysis reflect actual history as of late 1979 and DRI forecasts for the period following.

Table 4–2. Summary of no-energy-trouble (1973–1978) scenario.

	1973	1974	1975	1976	1977	1978
			Inflation Rates			
Core inflation rate	5.0	5.6	6.3	6.7	6.9	7.1
Shock inflation rate	2.6	1.1	0.3	0.4	0.3	0.9
Demand inflation rate	−1.9	1.2	1.2	−1.7	−1.1	−0.5
			Year-over-year Percentage Changes			
Real GNP	5.6	−0.4	1.3	6.0	4.4	4.4
Total consumption	4.7	−0.2	3.8	6.3	4.6	4.7
Nonres. fixed invest.	12.5	1.5	−8.5	5.9	6.4	8.0
Invest. in res. structures	−3.5	−19.7	−4.6	13.6	13.7	8.2
Net exports (level)	9.1	17.7	25.9	19.0	12.6	9.9
Government purchases	−0.2	2.2	2.5	0.9	2.5	1.9
Imported fuel price	4.2	5.5	5.5	5.5	5.5	5.5
Personal consumption deflator	5.1	7.8	5.9	4.1	4.9	6.2
Output per hour	2.1	−1.2	2.2	2.6	1.8	1.0
Potential GNP	4.2	3.4	3.6	3.2	3.1	3.4
			Percentage Points			
Unemployment rate	4.8	5.4	7.5	6.4	6.3	5.5

To assess the impact of the second OPEC shock, the most recent DRI macro forecast and recent history are contrasted with the hypothetical history shown by a solution that assumes continuing moderate energy price behavior. Table 4–5 shows that the second OPEC shock considerably worsened the economic outlook. Inflation in the years 1979–1981 is higher by an average of 0.9 percentage points a year, and the core inflation rate, the legacy we leave to the future, is worsened by over one-half of a percentage point by the end of 1981. Real activity is curtailed, and the unemployment rate is boosted by an average of 0.9 percentage points for 1980 and 1981.

A simulation has also been developed to calculate the total effects of both OPEC shocks and domestic price decontrol. Table 4–6 summarizes the results. By 1985, the cumulative effects of the energy crisis will have cost 10 percent of real activity and 5 percent of potential output and will have added almost 15 percent to the price

Table 4–3.   Economic impact of the first round of OPEC price increases: no-energy-trouble (1973–1978) compared to tracking simulation.

	1973	1974	1975	1976	1977	1978
	Difference in Percentage Points					
Core inflation rate	0.0	−0.3	−0.7	−0.9	−1.0	−1.0
Shock inflation rate	−0.3	−2.7	−0.9	−0.3	−0.5	−0.2
Demand inflation rate	0.0	0.0	0.3	0.7	0.8	0.5
	Percentage Difference					
Real GNP	0.1	1.1	3.8	4.0	3.1	3.1
Total consumption	0.0	0.7	2.7	3.1	2.7	2.9
Nonres. fixed invest.	0.2	1.9	7.4	8.4	6.0	5.4
Invest. in res. structures	0.5	7.5	19.0	9.6	3.2	7.3
Net exports (level)	19.3	12.1	15.2	20.3	22.1	−8.0
Government purchases	0.0	0.2	0.7	1.4	1.9	2.0
Imported fuel price	−27.9	−77.8	−78.9	−79.3	−79.7	−79.1
Personal consumption						
deflator	−0.4	−3.1	−5.1	−5.9	−6.6	−7.1
Output per hour	0.2	2.4	2.7	1.7	1.6	1.7
Potential GNP	0.0	0.1	0.5	1.0	1.6	2.0
	Difference in Percentage Points					
Unemployment rate	0.0	−0.2	−1.0	−1.3	−0.8	−0.5

level. The core inflation rate is worsened by an average of 0.9 percentage points over the entire period.

VI. ENERGY SHOCKS, DEMAND MANAGEMENT, AND CORE INFLATION

In the DRI intermediate-term forecast, the average rate of shock inflation for the years 1980–1985 is 1.6 percent. The shock rate is composed of a 1.1 percent energy component, where the forecast assumes a real rate of increase in OPEC prices of 5 percent a year, or a nominal rate of 13.8 percent, and the current domestic price decontrol policies for oil and gas are assumed to be allowed to be

Table 4-4.   Energy inflation after two rounds of OPEC price
increases (*total percentage change*).

	First OPEC Shock 1973-1976	Second OPEC Shock (History and Forecast) 1978-1981
OPEC marker price	60.0	41.4
Average U.S. import price	53.9	41.1
Average domestic oil price	18.5	56.0
Wholesale prices		
Fuels and power	25.5	35.3
Coal	19.1	7.5
Gas fuels	31.3	29.9
Electric power	17.1	15.3
Crude petroleum	26.2	48.1
Refined petroleum	29.0	44.4
Real prices, fuels, and power	10.9	16.0
All industrial commodities	13.2	16.6
Consumption deflators		
Household energy prices	15.2	32.4
Gasoline and motor oil	14.7	45.5
Fuel oil	22.3	40.4
Electricity	12.6	11.9
Gas	16.2	20.4
Real energy prices	6.7	19.6
All consumer prices	8.0	10.7

effective. Other elements in the projected shock include the sizeable payroll tax increase scheduled for 1981 and further annual increases thereafter. Food price increases are assumed to average out to close to a no-net shock contribution. The exchange rate is assumed to drop at a rate of 1 percent a year, given the current policies of rising outlays for oil imports and the disparity between our core inflation rate and those of the strong currency countries, Japan and West Germany.

The shock rate could be substantially worse, or even somewhat better. There is the possibility of a change in the world energy market for much better or much worse. The average experience on agri-

Table 4–5.   Economic impact of the second round of OPEC price increases: no-energy-trouble (1979–1985) compared to baseline case.

	1979	1980	1981	1982	1983	1984	1985
	Difference in Percentage Points						
Core inflation rate	0.0	−0.3	−0.5	−0.6	−0.7	−0.8	−0.8
Shock inflation rate	−0.9	−1.4	−0.7	−0.5	−0.4	−0.4	−0.4
Demand inflation rate	0.0	0.2	0.8	1.3	1.1	0.8	0.9
	Percentage Difference						
Real GNP	0.1	2.2	4.2	3.7	3.1	4.0	5.2
Total consumption	−0.1	1.1	2.6	2.6	2.3	2.8	3.6
Nonres. fixed invest.	0.3	3.4	7.5	6.8	4.3	5.0	7.6
Invest. in res. structures	1.7	15.3	19.9	9.4	5.4	11.2	16.0
Net exports (level)	4.4	13.6	13.7	12.8	17.3	21.8	24.8
Government purchases	0.1	1.0	2.4	3.3	3.8	4.1	4.7
Imported fuel price	−24.3	−41.2	−45.1	−48.6	−52.7	−56.1	−57.4
Personal consumption deflator	−1.1	−3.4	−4.9	−5.8	−6.4	−7.2	−8.0
Output per hour	0.6	2.6	2.7	2.0	1.7	2.5	3.1
Potential GNP	0.0	0.2	0.5	1.0	1.5	1.8	2.0
	Difference in Percentage Points						
Unemployment rate	0.0	−0.4	−1.3	−1.2	−0.7	−0.7	−1.1

cultural prices could be worse, and the government's ability to create other kinds of cost-raising shocks always remains considerable.

For the sake of illustration, the projected 1.6 percent shock rate is assumed. The change to aggregate demand is calculated as the amount required to produce the negative demand inflation effects that would offset the projected shock inflation. This exercise must be conducted over a time span of at least five years because the persistence in core inflation derived from the inflation expectations of workers and investors will dominate the results in the near term.

Tables 4–7 and 4–8 show the results of the demand-management exercise. The demand levers used were nonborrowed bank reserves (the principal operating tool of monetary policy), federal government defense and nondefense purchases, and federal government grants-in-aid to state and local governments. To reduce the core in-

Table 4–6. Total economic impact of two energy revolutions: no-energy trouble (1973–1985) compared to baseline case.

	1979	1980	1981	1982	1983	1984	1985
	Difference in Percentage Points						
Core inflation rate	−0.9	−1.0	−1.1	−1.0	−0.9	−0.9	−0.6
Shock inflation rate	−1.0	−1.4	−0.7	−0.5	−0.4	−0.4	−0.4
Demand inflation rate	0.6	0.6	1.0	1.3	1.0	0.6	0.7
	Percentage Difference						
Real GNP	3.3	6.0	8.0	7.5	7.7	9.1	10.1
Total consumption	3.0	4.4	5.9	5.7	5.9	6.9	7.6
Nonres. fixed invest.	6.3	10.2	14.5	13.4	11.2	12.5	14.6
Invest. in res. structures	11.1	24.7	25.3	15.3	14.8	21.0	24.3
Net exports (level)	−19.6	−3.1	−0.6	4.2	22.6	32.5	33.4
Government purchases	2.6	5.3	7.0	8.1	8.7	9.2	9.8
Imported fuel price	−83.9	−87.5	−88.3	−89.1	−89.9	−90.7	−90.9
Personal consumption deflator	−8.4	−10.7	−12.3	−13.0	−13.5	−14.1	−14.5
Output per hour	2.6	4.8	4.7	4.2	4.2	5.1	5.6
Potential GNP	2.4	2.6	2.9	3.5	4.0	4.4	4.7
	Difference in Percentage Points						
Unemployment rate	−0.4	−0.9	−1.7	−1.7	−1.3	−1.5	−1.9

flation rate by about 1 percentage point from a baseline path, unemployment must be increased by 2 percentage points for the years 1982–1985, and the utilization rate of the materials industries must be held down by 5 percentage points for most of the five-year period. To bring the core inflation rate down by about 3½ percentage points by the fiscal year 1985, the unemployment rate must be boosted by nearly 5 percentage points on top of the baseline projections.

If the shock inflation rate proves even worse, the requisite demand-management policies needed to prevent the core inflation rate from steadily rising would become truly prohibitive. An OPEC price increase of 10 percent a year in real terms would produce a shock inflation rate that would average over 2 percent for the years 1980–1985, sharply lifting the base from which any demand-management policy must begin.

Table 4–7.   Economic impact of lowering core inflation by 1 percent through demand management: reduced-demand scenario compared to baseline case.

	1979	1980	1981	1982	1983	1984	1985
	Difference in Percentage Points						
Core inflation rate	0.0	0.1	−0.2	−0.5	−1.0	−1.3	−1.2
Shock inflation rate	0.0	0.0	0.0	−0.1	−0.1	−0.2	−0.2
Demand inflation rate	0.0	−0.1	−0.7	−1.2	−1.5	−1.7	−1.5
	Percentage Difference						
Real GNP	0.0	−2.2	−4.3	−5.6	−5.8	−5.8	−5.6
Total consumption	0.0	−1.7	−3.7	−5.3	−6.0	−6.2	−6.1
Nonres. fixed invest.	0.0	−1.7	−5.4	−5.7	−4.5	−3.6	−2.6
Invest. in res. structures	−0.2	−10.5	−17.2	−7.9	−4.4	−6.3	−4.0
Net exports (level)	−0.1	9.6	29.7	50.4	68.9	67.7	51.9
Government purchases	0.0	−3.1	−4.6	−8.9	−10.7	−10.7	−10.3
Imported fuel price	0.0	−0.1	−0.3	−0.7	−1.4	−2.5	−3.6
Personal consumption deflator	0.0	0.0	−0.1	−0.4	−1.0	−2.0	−3.0
Output per hour	0.0	−1.0	−1.6	−1.8	−1.7	−1.5	−1.3
Potential GNP	0.0	0.0	−0.1	−0.4	−0.8	−1.0	−1.1
	Difference in Percentage Points						
Unemployment rate	0.0	0.5	1.5	2.0	2.1	2.0	1.9

These results show that the core inflation problem cannot be solved by aggregate demand policies.[5] The required unemployment paths are both politically unlikely and economically dangerous. The unemployment rates of disadvantaged groups and of disadvantaged regions (including central cities) would be dramatically higher. The economy would cease to be an engine of opportunity and progress, and the political process would surely opt for a worsening of inflation rather than for its cure.

Policy must turn to other techniques to lower the core inflation rate. DRI is conducting various studies[6] to explore the other possibilities, particularly various forms of investment tax incentives to accelerate capital formation and to restore a more normal productivity advance. Even with good, strong policies, the road ahead will not be easy.

Table 4–8.   Economic impact of lowering core inflation by 3–5 percent through demand management: reduced-demand scenario compared to baseline case.

	1979	1980	1981	1982	1983	1984	1985
			Difference in Percentage Points				
Core inflation rate	0.0	0.1	−0.2	−1.2	−2.3	−3.1	−3.8
Shock inflation rate	0.0	0.0	−0.1	−0.2	−0.4	−0.5	−0.7
Demand inflation rate	0.0	−0.2	−1.2	−2.4	−3.1	−3.4	−3.6
			Percentage Difference				
Real GNP	0.0	−3.4	−9.6	−12.5	−12.7	−14.8	−17.7
Total consumption	0.0	−2.8	−8.2	−11.5	−12.9	−15.4	−18.3
Nonres. fixed invest.	0.0	−2.3	−10.6	−13.9	−9.1	−7.2	−9.4
Invest. in res. structures	−0.2	−13.5	−35.7	−26.6	−12.5	−19.9	−21.1
Net exports (level)	−0.1	13.9	61.2	105.2	139.7	160.7	153.4
Government purchases	0.0	−4.8	−11.6	−18.2	−23.8	−27.8	−31.2
Imported fuel price	0.0	−0.1	−0.8	−2.0	−4.2	−7.3	−10.7
Personal consumption deflator	0.0	0.0	−0.2	−1.2	−3.2	−5.8	−8.8
Output per hour	0.0	−1.4	−3.6	−3.9	−3.2	−3.6	−4.2
Potential GNP	0.0	0.0	−0.2	−0.6	−1.3	−1.7	−2.0
			Difference in Percentage Points				
Unemployment rate	0.0	0.7	3.2	5.1	5.2	5.6	7.0

TECHNICAL APPENDIX TO CHAPTER 4

Energy Linkages in the DRI U.S. Macro Model

The 1979 version of the DRI U.S. Macro Model contains a significant expansion of energy-related detail and linkages. The price disaggregation is much greater and more precise than in previous versions; the role of energy quantities is enhanced, with a modeling of domestic demand and production permitting the calculation of imports endogenously; the modeling of energy-related consumption categories has been altered to more accurately reflect the post–OPEC energy world.

The macro model now contains the following energy-related concepts (asterisks denote new variables):

PMCRUDE*   The OPEC marker price for light Arabian crude oil, including the average surcharge after the first quarter of 1979.

JMEND10   The unit value index for imported fuels and lubricants.

PDOMCRUDE*   The domestic wellhead price for crude oil.

WPI051*   coal
WPI053*   natural gas
WPI054*   electricity   WPI05   Five components of the wholesale price index for fuels and related products and power.
WPI0561* crude oil
WPI057*   petroleum products

PCNGAS   Gasoline and motor oil
PCNFUEL   Home heating fuel   Price deflators for consumer purchases of fuels and related products and power.
PCSHHOPE   Electricity
PCSHHOPG   Natural gas

DTFUELSALLB* Total domestic energy demand, in Btu equivalents.

JQIND13*   Domestic oil and natural-gas production.

MEND1067   Imported quantity of fuels and lubricants.

The major exogenous levers are the domestic and imported-crude prices (PDOMCRUDE and PMCRUDE), domestic production (JQIND13), and the nonoil wholesale energy price components (WPI051, WPI053, and WPI054). Each of these concepts is modeled by a simulation rule wherein the primary determining variable is an exogenous counterpart. Equations derived from applicable theory, rather than regression analysis, cause the answers for these variables to differ from their exogenous counterparts when important related factors, such as the overall economy's inflation rate, change.

Other exogenous levers include, for electricity prices, the share of coal, petroleum, and natural gas as source fuels in electricity production (EUF%COAL, EUF%PET, and EUF%NG); for domestic crude prices, the proportion of domestic crude oil production that is subject to price regulation (REG%DOMOILPROD); for petroleum product prices, the domestically produced share of domestic oil demand (DOM%OIL); for retail gasoline prices, the average governmental tax per gallon on gasoline (GASTAX); and for oil imports, the share of petroleum and natural gas in aggregate domestic energy demand (PET&NG%ENERGY).

I. THE PRICE BLOCK

Determination of primary energy prices is largely exogenous. Attempts to model their behavior through regression analysis proved problematical because (a) OPEC actions and regulatory developments are not easily captured, and (b) the energy sector is in a period of rapid structural change, which regression techniques cannot handle adequately. Consequently, the current DRI approach uses exogenously determined values for key prices, with simulation rules (nonstochastic equations) used to capture the impact on energy prices of other prices, regulatory developments, mix changes, and structural changes.

Petroleum Prices

Oil prices are primarily determined by appropriate weighting of domestic (PDOMCRUDE) and imported (PMCRUDE) crude prices.

The imported price variable is the OPEC price, expressed in dollars per barrel (PMCRUDE). Through the first quarter of 1979 the data are set at the pretransportation price for Saudi Arabian marker (light) crude. The March 26, 1979 OPEC meeting effectively changed the marker crude price from a ceiling price to a base price. Therefore, after the first quarter of 1979, adjustments are made to PMCRUDE to reflect the base price plus an average surcharge. The values are still meant to capture the price of a crude of similar quality to the Saudi light for consistency with the historical data. Since it is difficult to separate premium differentials from surcharges, the price value becomes a best approximation and not an actually quoted price.

This variable (PMCRUDE) is the lever for simulating OPEC price increases. Use of this lever, rather than JMEND10 (as in previous model versions) or PMCRUDEEXO, will ensure that changes flow through appropriately. (Changes made to JMEND10 will affect the trade deficit, and thus GNP, without affecting energy prices; changes to PMCRUDEEXO will affect energy prices without affecting the trade deficit.)

PMCRUDE is determined exogenously, with a simulation rule to reflect changes in domestic demand prices:

$$PMCRUDE = PMCRUDEEXO*PC\&I\&G/PC\&I\&GEXO,$$

where PC&I&G is the composite implicit price deflator for domestic demand (consumption, investment, and government purchases), and PMCRUDEEXO and PC&I&GEXO are exogenized counterparts of the corresponding variables. This formulation assumes that OPEC prices are determined partially by U.S. inflation developments. Their prices are not assumed to respond to exchange-rate changes, since OPEC prices are, at least in the short run, denominated in dollars.

In standard DRI solutions, PC&I&GEXO, an exogenous variable, is set equal to the value of PC&I&G, so the last two terms on the righthand side of the equation cancel, and PMCRUDE equals PMCRUDEEXO.

A simple bridge equation is employed to translate the imported crude oil price into the unit value index for imported fuel (JMEND–10). This index is used in deriving the fuel import bill in the trade sector (MEND10). It forms no other linkages with the macro economy, since PMCRUDE is the channel through which all other links are defined. Several important considerations about the nature of the data for JMEND10 should be clarified:

1. JMEND10 is obtained from the Bureau of the Census publication FT900, and derived as follows:

    $$\% \Delta \text{JMEND10} = \% \Delta (\text{MPETNS}/\text{MQPETNS})$$

where:

MPETNS   = value of U.S. petroleum imports, F.A.S.,
                     $/quarter

MQPETNS = quantity of U.S. petroleum imports, millions
                     of barrels per day (mmbd)/quarter.

2. Movement in JMEND10 captures the movement in prices of all the fuels we import. Hence quality and mix changes will be included, in contrast to PMCRUDE, which captures just the movement in prices of a particular grade of crude oil.
3. The imports are valued F.A.S.; hence prices will be slightly higher than the transaction cost reflected in PMCRUDE, but lower than if valued C.I.F. or on a refiner's acquisition basis. Recent data for JMEND10 were consistent with the following prices per barrel:

	1977	1978	1979
$/barrel	13.32	13.31	18.77
Percentage change	9.4	−0.1	41.0

4. The import category includes all fuel imports. Hence rising natural-gas imports may provide another source of discontinuity between JMEND10 and PMCRUDE in the future.

   An approach similar to that for PMCRUDE is utilized for domestic wellhead crude prices, except that the inflation factor is separated out: The regulated portion of domestic production can, in a simulation, change only when domestic inflation changes, since the regulations generally set ceiling prices that are a function of a base price and an inflation markup. The nonregulated portion, on the other hand, moves at the world oil price (approximated by PMCRUDE). The exogenous share variable REG%DOMOILPROD, which represents the controlled share of domestic production, controls how much the composite domestic crude-oil prices will change with respect to both domestic price inflation and world oil prices:

$$PDOMCRUDE = PDOMCRUDEEXO * (REG\%DOMOILPROD * PC\&I\&G /$$
$$PC\&I\&GEXO$$
$$+ (1 - REG\%DOMOILPROD) * PMCRUDE / PMCRUDEEXO).$$

Domestic wholesale crude-oil prices (WPI0561) are determined by simulation rule from the composite domestic crude-oil price:

$$WPI0561 = WPI0561EXO * PDOMCRUDE / PDOMCRUDEEXO.$$

Domestic petroleum product prices (WPI057) are determined by simulation rules from domestic wholesale crude-oil prices and the OPEC marker price for crude. The exogenous share variable DOM% OIL determines the proportion of petroleum product prices that reflects passthrough of OPEC prices and the proportion that reflects passthrough of domestic crude-oil prices. The simulation rule assumes a distributed lag adjustment of refined product prices to crude-oil input prices:

$$WPI057 = WPI057EXO *$$

$$\sum_{i=0}^{3} a_i \left(DOM\%OIL_{-i} * \frac{WPI0561_{-i}}{WPI0561EXO_{-i}} + (1 - DOM\%OIL_{-i}) * \frac{PMCRUDE_{-i}}{PMCRUDEEXO_{-i}} \right)$$

$$a_i = 0.2, 0.4, 0.3, 0.1 \qquad \Sigma a_i = 1.0$$

Consumer gasoline prices (PCNGAS) are estimated net of federal, state, and local taxes. According to DOE, approximately 2.7 percent of U.S. gasoline is imported; therefore, an input cost term is constructed by weighting wholesale refined petroleum product prices (WPI057) and imported crude-oil prices (PMCRUDE):

$$gascost = 0.973 * WPI057 + 0.027 * PMCRUDE / 1.710,$$

where the 1.710 constant converts the dollar-per-barrel PMCRUDE term to a 1967-based index for consistency with the WPI term. The gas price equation is then estimated as:

$$\log \left(\frac{gasprice}{gasprice_{-1}} \right) = \underset{(0.002)}{0.00102} - \underset{(0.004)}{0.00703 * DMYPRICE}$$

$$+ \underset{(0.047)}{0.731} * \log \left(\frac{gascost}{gascost_{-1}} \right)$$

$\bar{R}^2$ = 0.7981 (normalized on PCNGAS, $\bar{R}^2$ = 0.9982).

D.W. = 2.05

S.E.E. = 0.016 (normalized on PCNGAS, S.E.E. = 0.014)
      with gasprice defined as:

gasprice = PCNGAS − GASTAX/36.130,

where 36.130 is the average price, in 1972 cents, of one gallon of gasoline, and GASTAX is the average tax per gallon, in cents.

Consumer home heating-fuel prices (PCNFUEL) are estimated in rate of change form from an input cost term derived from domestic petroleum product prices (WPI057), imported petroleum product prices (proxied by PMCRUDE), and unit labor costs (TEMP@JULCNF):

$$fuelcost = 0.8 * (0.955 * WPI057 + 0.045 * PMCRUDE/1.7)$$
$$+ 0.2 * TEMP@JULCNF$$

The weights for domestic and imported product prices were derived from DOE data, and represent the shares of domestic and imported petroleum products in home heating-fuel supplies. The estimated equation is:

$$\log \left(\frac{PCNFUEL}{PCNFUEL_{-1}} \right) = \underset{(0.028)}{0.952} * \log \left(\frac{fuelcost}{fuelcost_{-1}} \right)$$

$\bar{R}^2$ = 0.8732 (normalized on PCNFUEL, $\bar{R}^2$ = 0.9988).

D.W. = 1.61

S.E.E. = 0.013 (normalized on PCNFUEL, S.E.E. = 0.020)

Coal Prices

Wholesale spot coal prices (WPI051) are determined exogenously, with a simulation rule that effects a 100 percent feedthrough of domestic inflation:

$$WPI051 = WPI051EXO*PC\&I\&G/PC\&I\&GEXO.$$

The price used in construction of the index by the Bureau of Labor Statistics is the spot price. Coal moving under the contract is not considered. Coke prices (WPI052), which form a very small part of the total fuel price index, are not explicitly modeled. In input-output calculations of fuel cost indices for other industries, and in the calculation of the aggregate index (WPI05), the weights that would accrue to WPI052 were assigned instead to coal prices (WPI051).

Natural-Gas Prices

Wholesale wellhead natural-gas prices (WPI053) are determined exogenously, with a simulation rule that effects a 100 percent feedthrough of domestic inflation:

$$WPI053 = WPI053EXO*PC\&I\&G/PC\&I\&GEXO.$$

This simulation rule captures the tie-in of price ceilings, established under the Natural Gas Deregulation Act, to the inflation rate.

Consumer natural-gas prices (PCSHHOPG) are determined from wholesale prices (WPI053) and unit labor costs (TEMP@JULCNF):

$$\log\left(\frac{PCSHHOPG}{PCSHHOPG_{-1}}\right) = \begin{array}{c} -0.000396 \\ (0.001673) \end{array} + \begin{array}{c} 0.583*\log\left(\frac{TEMP@JULCNF_{-1}}{TEMP@JULCNF_{-2}}\right) \\ (0.146) \end{array}$$

$$+ \sum_{i=1}^{3} a_i * \log\left(\frac{WPI053_{-i}}{WPI053_{-i-1}}\right)$$

$$a_i = 0.0996, 0.1133, 0.1012, 0.0635$$

$$\Sigma a_i = \begin{array}{c} 0.378 \\ (0.042) \end{array}$$

$\bar{R}^2$ = 0.7545 (normalized on PCSHHOPG, $\bar{R}^2$ = 0.9992)

D.W. = 1.67

S.E.E. = 0.0086 (normalized on PCSHHOPG, S.E.E. = 0.011)

Electricity Prices

Wholesale electricity prices (WPI054) are determined by the costs of the three primary input fuels (coal, petroleum, and natural gas), and the proportions of generation fuel accounted for by each source. The exogenous weight EUF%COAL applies to the coal spot price WPI051; the exogenous weight EUF%NG applies to the natural-gas price WPI053; the exogenous weight EUF%PET applies to the petroleum product price WPI057. The weights sum to less than one, reflecting the remaining sources of fuel (primarily nuclear and hydro). The simulation rule that generates wholesale electricity prices is based on a distributed lag formula:

$$\frac{WPI054}{WPI054EXO} = \sum_{i=0}^{3} w_i * \left(EUF\%COAL_{-i} * \frac{WPI051_{-i}}{WPI051EXO_{-i}} \right.$$

$$+ \ EUF\%NG_{-i} * \frac{WPI053_{-i}}{WPI053EXO_{-i}} + EUF\%PET_{-i} * \frac{WPI057_{-i}}{WPI57EXO_{-i}}$$

$$+ \left. (1 - EUF\%COAL_{-i} - EUF\%NG_{-i} - EUF\%PET_{-i}) \right)$$

$w_0 = 0.2, \ w_1 = 0.4, \ w_2 = 0.3, \ w_3 = 0.1$

Consumer electricity prices (PCSHHOPE) are determined by the wholesale price. A dummy variable was used in the estimation to account for the effects of price controls during the Nixon administration:

$$\log \left(\frac{PCSHHOPE}{PCSHHOPE_{-1}} \right) = \underset{(0.080)}{0.633} * \log \left(\frac{WPI054}{WPI054_{-1}} \right)$$

$$+ \underset{(0.0779)}{0.0957} * \log \left(\frac{WPI054_{-1}}{WPI054_{-2}} \right) - \underset{(0.0020)}{0.00345} * DMYPRICE$$

$\bar{R}^2$ = 0.7295 (normalized on PCSHHOPE, $\bar{R}^2$ = 0.9985)

D.W. = 1.63

S.E.E. = 0.0077 (normalized on PCSHHOPE, S.E.E. = 0.011)

Aggregate Wholesale Price Index (Fuels)

WPI05, the wholesale price index for fuels and related products, is calculated from the components represented in the model, mainly using the relative weights of the index. A time trend is necessary to correct for shifting weights of the index and for the assignment of coke to the coal category. Then, assigning the weight for coke prices to coal prices (WPI051), the following equation was estimated:

WPI05 = −0.0201 + 0.995 * weightedsum
         (0.0019)   (0.0038)

         + 0.00315 * log (t) * weightedsum
         (0.00077)

$\bar{R}^2$ = 1.0000

D.W. = 0.52

S.E.E. = 0.0042

where weightedsum = 0.05281*WPI051+0.11341*WPI053+ 0.28158*WPI054+0.09466*WPI0561+0.47452*WPI057 and t = TIME−60 is a time trend.

II. THE DEMAND BLOCK

The energy demand block centers on four consumption equations— gasoline, home heating fuel, electricity, and natural gas—and a total energy demand equation.

Gasoline

Gasoline consumption is estimated on a per-capita basis in log-linear form. The determining variables are real per-capita disposable income, with a four-period linear lag structure; a four-period moving average of the per-capita automobile stock; the average miles per gallon achieved by new model-year cars; and the relative price of gasoline, with a four-period linear lag structure:

$$\log\left(\frac{CNGAS72}{N}\right) = \begin{array}{c} -1.94 \\ (0.36) \end{array} + \begin{array}{c} 0.485 \\ (0.145) \end{array} * \log\left(\sum_{i=0}^{3} w_i * \frac{YD72_{-i}}{N_{-i}}\right)$$

$$+ \begin{array}{c} 0.733 \\ (0.168) \end{array} * \log\left(\frac{1}{4*N} * \sum_{i=1}^{4} KREGCARS_{-i}\right)$$

$$- \begin{array}{c} 0.0769 \\ (0.0537) \end{array} * \log(AVGMPG)$$

$$- \sum_{j=0}^{4} w_j * \log\left(\frac{PCNGAS_{-j}}{PC_j}\right)$$

$w_i = 0.4, 0.3, 0.2, 0.1$ $\Sigma w_i = 1.0$

$w_j = 0.104, 0.083, 0.062, 0.042, 0.021$ $\Sigma w_j = 0.312 \ (0.069)$

$\overline{R}^2 = 0.9802$ (normalized on CNGAS72, $\overline{R}^2 = 0.9882$)

D.W. = 0.47

S.E.E. = 0.028 (normalized on CNGAS72, S.E.E. = 0.558)

The relevant elasticities are thus 0.485 for income, 0.733 for the car stock, −0.104 for relative price in the short run, and −0.312 for relative price in the long run.

Heating Fuel

Home heating-fuel consumption is estimated on a per-housing-unit basis, in log-linear form. The determining variables are real disposable income, with a low elasticity (0.209), the relative price, with a long-run elasticity of −0.336, and consumer sentiment. The small size of this data series, relative to the precision to which the data are reported, and the effects of weather on heating-fuel consumption, make accurate modeling difficult and R-squareds low; however, the standard error is a very modest $0.25 billion.

$$\log\left(\frac{\text{CNFUEL72}}{\text{KQHUSTS}_{-1}}\right) = \underset{(0.23)}{-3.77} + \underset{(0.036)}{0.209} * \log\left(\sum_{i=0}^{3} w_i * \text{YD72}_{-i}\right)$$

$$+ \sum_{j=2}^{4}\left(w_j * \log\left(\text{JATTC}_{-j}\right)\right)$$

$$- \sum_{k=0}^{4}\left(w_k * \log\left(\frac{\text{PCNFUEL}_{-k}}{\text{PC}_{-k}}\right)\right)$$

w_i = 0.4, 0.3, 0.2, 0.1 Σw_i = 1.0

w_j = 0.101, 0.151, 0.117 Σw_j = 0.368 (0.059)

w_k = 0.112, 0.090, 0.067, 0.045, 0.022 Σw_k = 0.336 (0.040)

$\overline{R}^2$ = 0.7028 (normalized on CNFUEL72, $\overline{R}^2$ = 0.7841)

D.W. = 1.22

S.E.E. = 0.046 (normalized on CNFUEL72, S.E.E. = 0.254)

Electricity

Electricity consumption is modeled as a per-housing-unit function of income, relative price, and consumer sentiment, in log-linear form. Transfer income is separated from nontransfer income; the resulting response of electricity consumption is more immediate for transfer income. The estimated price elasticity is a modest −0.213 on a given housing stock:

$$\log\left(\frac{\text{CSHHOPE72}}{\text{KQHUSTSMH}_{-1}}\right) = \underset{(0.07)}{5.85} + \underset{(0.014)}{0.394} * \log\left(\sum_{i=0}^{3} w_i\left(\frac{\text{YD}_{-i} - \text{VG}_{-i}}{\text{PC}_{-i}}\right)\right)$$

$$+ \underset{(0.011)}{0.332} * \log\left(\frac{\text{VG}_{-1}}{\text{PC}_{-1}}\right)$$

$$- \sum_{j=0}^{4}\left(w_j * \log\left(\frac{\text{PCSHHOPE}_{-j}}{\text{PC}_{-j}}\right)\right)$$

$$+ \sum_{k=1}^{5}\left(w_k * \log\left(\text{JATTC}_{-k}\right)\right)$$

$$w_i = 0.4,\ 0.3,\ 0.2,\ 0.1 \qquad\qquad \Sigma w_i = 1.0$$

$$w_j = 0.071,\ 0.057,\ 0.043,\ 0.028,\ 0.014 \qquad \Sigma w_j = 0.213\ (0.030)$$

$$w_k = 0.034,\ 0.031,\ 0.027,\ 0.020,\ 0.011 \qquad \Sigma w_k = 0.123\ (0.033)$$

$\bar{R}^2 = 0.9896$ (normalized on CSHHOPE72, $\bar{R}^2 = 0.9921$)

D.W. = 1.40

S.E.E. = 0.022 (normalized on CSHHOPE72, S.E.E. = 0.290)

Natural Gas

Natural-gas consumption is estimated as a per-housing-unit function of disposable income, relative price, and consumer sentiment. The income elasticity is a modest 0.387; the long-run price elasticity is −0.339. The explanatory power of the equation is limited, like the heating-fuel equation, by the size and imprecision of the series, and the lack of an appropriate weather variable.

$$\log\left(\frac{CSHHOPG72}{KQHUSTS_{-1}}\right) = \underset{(0.23)}{4.95} + \underset{(0.036)}{0.387} * \log\left(\sum_{i=0}^{3} w_i * YD72_{-i}\right)$$

$$- \sum_{j=0}^{4} w_j * \log\left(\frac{PCSHHOPG_{-j}}{PC_{-j}}\right)$$

$$+ \sum_{k=1}^{4} w_k * \log\left(JATTC_{-k}\right)$$

$$w_i = 0.4,\ 0.3,\ 0.2,\ 0.1 \qquad\qquad \Sigma w_i = 1.0$$

$$w_j = 0.113,\ 0.090,\ 0.068,\ 0.045,\ 0.023 \qquad \Sigma w_j = 0.339\ (0.042)$$

$$w_k = 0.060,\ 0.054,\ 0.042,\ 0.024 \qquad\qquad \Sigma w_k = 0.180\ (0.063)$$

$\bar{R}^2 = 0.6887$ (normalized on CSHHOPG72, $\bar{R}^2 = 0.8852$)

D.W. = 1.30

S.E.E. = 0.050 (normalized on CSHHOPG72, S.E.E. = 0.295)

Total Energy Demand

Total U.S. energy demand is modeled in Btu equivalents as a function of consumer energy demands, industrial activity, and relative price. The consumer demand term is defined as:

$$consumerdemand = CNGAS72+CNFUEL72+CSHHOPE72+CSHHOPG72 \\ +a*CSTRANS72,$$

where a represents the share of transportation services that is energy. This share is estimated as a function of a time trend. Specifying industrial demand for energy as a function of industrial production in manufacturing (JQINDM), mining (JQINDMI), and utilities (JQIND49&G), and defining the relative price term as the ratio of the wholesale price index for fuels and related products and power (WPI05) to the aggregate wholesale price index (WPI), we estimate total demand for energy, in quadrillion Btu (DTFUELSALLB), as follows:

$$
\begin{aligned}
\log (DTFUELSALLB) =\ & 1.744 \\
& (0.252) \\
& +0.613 * \log (consumerdemand) \\
& (0.066) \\
& +0.101 * \log (JQINDM) \\
& (0.025) \\
& +0.087 * \log (JQIND49\&G) \\
& (0.050) \\
& +0.114 * \log (JQINDMI) \\
& (0.055) \\
& -\sum_{i=1}^{5} w_i * \log (relativeprice_{-i})
\end{aligned}
$$

w_i = 0.023, 0.019, 0.014, 0.009, 0.005 Σw_i = 0.070 (0.010)

$\overline{R}^2$ = 0.9974 (normalized on DTFUELSALLB, $\overline{R}^2$ = 0.9970)

D.W. = 1.18

S.E.E. = 0.009 (normalized on DTFUELSALLB, S.E.E. = 0.601)

The coefficients on the relative price terms cannot be directly interpreted as elasticities, since the consumer demand term already has price elasticity effects built in. Similarly, the full-system elasticities on the industrial production terms are not equal to the corresponding coefficients except for movements in the particular index that are independent of movements in the other two indices and in the consumer energy demand categories.

III. THE SUPPLY BLOCK

The energy supply block takes domestic crude-oil and natural-gas production (JQIND13) as exogenous, and calculates oil and gas imports (MEND1067) as a residual type of energy supply. That is to say, an increase in domestic energy demand will, in the short run, be met primarily by the importation of additional foreign oil.

Domestic Supply

Production of oil and natural gas is represented by the variable JQIND13 from the Federal Reserve Board's Industrial Production series. It is a subset of the mining composite, comprising in the base period (1967) 69.2 percent of all mining and 4.4 percent of all industrial production. It includes the following major components:

	Percentage of JQIND13	Percentage of JQIND
Oil and gas extraction (JQIND13)	100.0	4.4
Crude oil	66.7	2.9
Natural-gas liquids	6.8	0.3
Natural gas	15.2	0.7
Oil and gas drilling	11.3	0.5

In the model, JQIND13 is forecast exogenously; a simulation rule allows for a small (0.05) short-run and moderate (0.44) long-run supply elasticity, based on domestic wellhead crude-oil prices:

$$\log \left(\frac{\text{JQIND13}}{\text{JQIND13EXO}} \right) = \sum_{i=0}^{24} w_i * \log \left(\frac{\text{PDOMCRUDE}_{-i}}{\text{PDOMCRUDEEXO}_{-i}} \right)$$

w_i = 0.01 for i = 0–4, i = 10, and i = 24

w_i = 0.02 for i = 11, i = 23

w_i = 0.03 for i = 12–22

w_i = 0 for i = 5–9

Σw_i = 0.44

Import Supply

Energy imports to the United States are captured by the Bureau of Census value, in 1967 dollars, of all imports of fuels and lubricants (MEND1067). Although primarily crude oil and petroleum products, the series does include natural gas, other fuel imports, and lubricants. The fact must be remembered when translating oil imports of mmbd into constant-dollar imports (MEND1067). The census data are often at odds with either the levels, or the movement in levels, of oil import quantities available from the Department of Energy (DOE) and the American Petroleum Institute (API). For reference, the following benchmark figures for the oil import quantities associated with MEND1067 may be helpful:

	Oil Imports (mmbd)[a]		
	1977	1978	1979
Census	8.72	8.14	8.30
API	8.59	8.15	8.28
DOE	8.79	8.03	8.20
Strategic storage	0.02	0.16	0.07

[a]Millions of barrels per day.

It should be noted that the Census figures include imports for strategic storage, whereas the API figures do not; DOE provides estimates both with and without strategic storage. Furthermore, the sampling techniques and timing differ among the three estimates. None of the figures includes imports to the Virgin Islands; they appear in the statistical discrepancy to the trade accounts, STATM67.

The equation for imports of fuels and lubricants (primarily crude oil, refined petroleum products, and natural gas) is derived from total demand and total production. Total demand can be approximated historically by adding domestic production and imports, scaling the two concepts so they are in equivalent units:

$$\text{domestic (realized) demand} = a * \frac{\text{JQIND13}}{\text{JQIND13}\,[t]} + b * \frac{\text{MEND1067}}{\text{MEND1067}\,[t]},$$

where a is the domestic supply in some time period t, in mmbd, and b is the equivalent import supply. Choosing any year t, and the corresponding values for a and b, domestic demand is defined in barrel equivalents.

A relationship is assumed between domestic demand and total energy demand (DTFUELSALLB), multiplied by the petroleum and natural-gas share of total energy demand (PET&NG%ENERGY):

$$\log \text{(domestic demand)} = a_0 + a_1 * \log \text{(DTFUELSALLB*PET\&NG\%ENERGY)} +$$
$$a_2 * \text{TIME} + a_3 * \log \text{(TIME)} - a_4 * \log \text{(relative price)},$$

where the relative price is the cost of oil- and natural-gas-related fuels relative to the cost of all fuels. This can be approximated by constructing a measure similar to WPI05, but excluding coal and the nonpetroleum/natural-gas share of electricity:

$$\text{cost } oil/ng = (0.153*\text{WPI053} + 0.214*(\text{EUF\%NG} + \text{EUF\%PET})$$
$$*\text{WPI054} + 0.087*\text{WPI0561} + 0.478$$
$$*\text{WPI057})/(0.718 + 0.214*(\text{EUF\%PET} + \text{EUF\%NG}))$$

The equation was then estimated as:

$$\log \text{(domestic demand)} = 7.725 + 0.972 * \log \text{(DTFUELSALLB*PET\&NG\%}$$
$$(3.884)\quad(0.250)\qquad\qquad\qquad\qquad\text{ENERGY)}$$
$$+ 0.038 * \text{TIME}$$
$$(0.012)$$
$$-3.429 * \log \text{(TIME)} - \Sigma w_i \log \text{(relative price)}$$
$$(1.239)$$

w_i = 0.022, 0.043, 0.061, 0.078, 0.092, 0.105, 0.115, 0.124, 0.131, 0.136,
  0.139, 0.140, 0.139, 0.136, 0.131, 0.124, 0.115, 0.105, 0.092, 0.078, 0.061,
  0.043, 0.022 Σw_i = 2.23 (0.51)

$\bar{R}^2$ = 0.9411 (normalized on MEND1067, $\bar{R}^2$ = 0.9706)

D.W. = 1.34

S.E.E. = 0.0240 (normalized on MEND1067, S.E.E. = 0.333)

Given the definition of domestic demand (above), this estimated relationship can be arranged to solve for MEND1067.

The sum of the coefficients on the relative price term cannot be interpreted directly as a price elasticity because the numerator and denominator are not sufficiently independent; the true price elasticity is quite small.

NOTES TO CHAPTER 4

1. In this analysis, price controls on energy goods are assumed to be fully effective. This differs from the analysis in Chapter 3.
2. The version of the energy sector described here was developed by Frank Cooper, Douglas Rice, and Virginia Rogers of DRI.
3. For a fuller theoretical treatment of equilibrium price, see Nordhaus (1972).
4. The paper by Mork and Hall (1980b), which analyzes the same experience, has generally similar results.
5. This conclusion depends, of course, on the assumptions of the model, such as the expectation formation mechanism. However, similar results have also been reached in other studies using different models, such as Mork and Hall (1980a, 1980b, and Chapter 3 of this volume).
6. See U.S. Congress (1980).

5 ANALYSIS OF OIL PRICE SHOCKS IN THE MPS MODEL

Stephan Thurman
Richard Berner*

I. INTRODUCTION

Decisions on the appropriate fiscal and monetary policy responses to energy price increases require thorough analysis of their macroeconomic effects. This chapter focuses on the unique characteristics of energy price shocks for the U.S. economy and simulates the experienced and projected macroeconomic effects of OPEC price increases, using the M.I.T.–Penn–SSRC (MPS) econometric model. The standard channels of transmission of external inflationary shocks have been analyzed at length in previous MPS model studies by Pierce and Enzler (1974), Berner et al. (1975), and Thurman and Kwack (1976).[1] We review these mechanisms only briefly and concentrate instead on the special features of oil price increases.

The analysis carefully considers three types of energy prices: imported-oil prices, domestic oil production prices, and the wholesale price index for energy. Average imported-oil prices in the United States are calculated as a weighted average of prices charged by OPEC and non-OPEC exporting countries. Domestic oil production prices are calculated from upper-tier, lower-tier, marginal, and noncon-

*Economists, Board of Governors of the Federal Reserve System. The authors would like to acknowledge the helpful comments on versions of this paper provided by Flint Brayton, Jared Enzler, and John Kalchenbrenner, and the typing by Susan Eubank. The views expressed in this paper are solely those of the authors and do not necessarily represent the views of the board or its staff.

trolled oil prices at the wellhead.[2] Domestic wholesale energy prices, net of imported petroleum prices, are Btu-equivalent, output-weighted average prices of domestic oil, coal, natural gas, and other energy prices.[3]

The three prices are plotted as indexes (1972 = 100) in Figure 5–1, where the extension beyond the second quarter of 1979 represents the energy price paths anticipated from the June 1979 OPEC announcement of their scheduled oil export prices. Beyond 1979, this schedule is extended to approximate a slight real rate of growth in world oil prices. The two domestic price paths are closely linked to that for imported oil. These linkages will be discussed in detail below.

Two salient features of this figure are the discrete jumps in the world oil price in the 1974 and 1979 periods and the shapes of the paths of domestic energy prices, which are regulated below world energy prices in the 1974–1979 period and then phased up to world price levels in the 1979–1981 period. Domestic wholesale energy prices react slowly to world and domestic oil price increases due to long-term contract lags in the domestic nonoil energy–producing industries. Domestic refined petroleum product prices, which are also a component of the wholesale energy price index, rise toward world oil prices at an increasing rate as oil price controls are removed.

We will analyze the macroeconomic effects of the June 1979 OPEC price increase in contrast to the energy price assumptions used in a control forecast scenario prior to the increase. In addition, we consider two possible OPEC pricing alternatives. First, we examine the impact of denominating the dollar price of oil per barrel in terms of a basket of currencies rather than in dollars; and second, we analyze further discrete jumps in the OPEC price schedule beyond 1979. Both these alternatives would significantly raise the OPEC price path and thus the path of domestic oil and competing energy prices as they rise to world levels by 1981.

The organization of the analysis is as follows: Section II discusses the features of an oil price shock that distinguish it from the analysis of the standard transmission channels of imported inflation. Section III will explain the methodology used to calculate the domestic energy price changes, as well as the way these energy price changes feed through the MPS model presented in Section IV. Section V concludes by discussing the importance of the simulation results for monetary and fiscal policy.

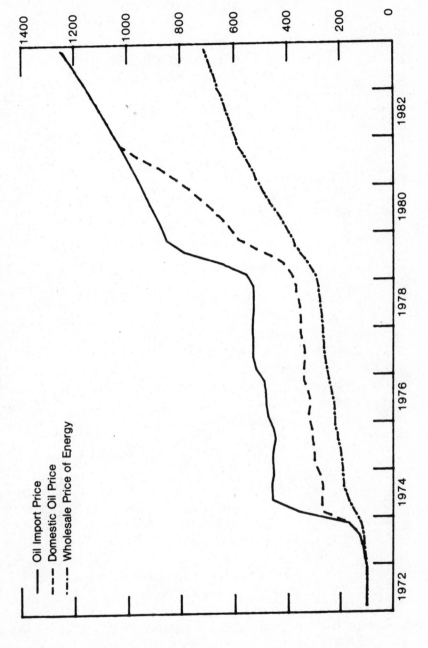

Figure 5–1. Energy prices in the United States (1972 = 100).

—— Oil Import Price
––– Domestic Oil Price
–·– Wholesale Price of Energy

II. TRANSMISSION CHANNELS
OF AN OIL PRICE SHOCK

The effects of any increase in import prices are transmitted to domestic prices through three standard channels. First, the increase
in import prices is passed through to the price of final sales, both
directly and indirectly, since imports are both final and intermediate
goods. Second, the prices of import-competing goods—in this case
domestic oil, coal, and natural gas—rise, and these price increases are
passed on similarly to final sales prices. Finally, the first two effects
on consumption prices result in higher wage demands, which set off
a wage–price spiral.

In addition to these standard transmission channels, the following
features are unique to oil price shocks.[4]

Demand and Supply Elasticities

While produced domestically, the supply elasticity of oil appears to
be very low, at least in the short run. This seems to be true of the
demand elasticity as well, whether oil is used as an intermediate input
or as a final product. The OPEC cartel, acting in its own best inter-
ests, has the political and economic power to keep prices high so long
as the cartel retains cohesion. Finally, many of the OPEC countries
do not want to, or cannot, exchange anything but a small fraction of
their receipts from the sale of oil for exports from the oil-importing
countries.

Since oil demand as well as domestic supply is relatively insensitive
to prices in the short run, a rise in oil prices means that total dollar
expenditures on imported oil will increase. If there is no change in
savings and nominal income, the higher oil import prices will result in
a decline in expenditures on domestic goods and services relative to
what would have occurred without the price rise. Oil price increases
have been likened to the imposition of a sales tax, the proceeds of
which are not spent immediately. This results in a net contractionary
effect on the economy because of a decline in aggregate demand. The
loss in real domestic income is a real income transfer to OPEC.

Energy, labor, and capital are all inputs used in production. As the
price of energy rises relative to other factor prices, producers will

tend to substitute away from energy toward the other factors. Since factor proportions are relatively fixed once capital is installed, most factor substitution will take place only when the capital is fully depreciated. Additionally, depending on the substitution elasticities, a rise in energy prices may tend to make producers substitute away from both capital and energy toward labor. By definition this implies lower labor productivity and less demand for new investment. In any case, the aggregate supply of output is reduced as a result of substitution away from energy.

World Prices and Activity

An increase in world oil prices increases inflation in other oil-importing countries.[5] Consequently, prices in U.S. trading-partner countries will also rise and their activity levels will fall as a result of the oil price increase. World trade as a whole will shift from nonenergy-related products and services to imported oil from oil-exporting countries. The net effect of this shift in the terms of trade of oil-importing countries will be a lowering of trade volume among oil-importing countries and a rise in prices of traded goods.

Ordinarily, if the world operated under a freely flexible exchange rate system, large changes in relative prices between countries would be offset by changes in exchange rates. The exchange rate outcomes of an oil price increase are complicated by the fact that they depend on the share of unspent oil revenues that OPEC countries wish to hold in the form of dollar-dominated financial claims. A very small percentage of OPEC revenues are used to purchase goods and services from oil-importing countries; the remainder is invested. If the members of OPEC decided to shift part of their assets from dollars to a foreign currency or a basket of foreign currencies, the resultant exchange rate impacts on U.S. inflation could be large. It is impossible to predict exchange rate changes following an oil price increase without knowing the distribution of the increase in OPEC wealth. As a further complication, the problem involves simultaneity: The willingness of the OPEC members to continue to hold their assets in dollars probably depends on their expectations of the dollar exchange rate, which in turn are related to U.S. inflation relative to that of other countries, and to U.S. monetary policy.

Inflationary Expectations

The discrete nature of oil price shocks affects inflationary expectations differently than do other sources of inflation. The timing of OPEC price hikes has been generally impossible to predict. Hence, the variance of inflationary expectations will be larger in a world of unpredictable oil price rises. Domestic output and expenditure patterns are difficult to plan when petroleum product supply sources behave erratically, as was the case with the interruption in world oil production during the Iranian revolution.

Energy Regulation and Control

Domestic petroleum supply and prices are subject to administered stockpiling and a complicated set of price regulations. These price controls, and the recently announced plans for phasing them out, introduce further complexity to the analysis of OPEC price shocks. Under the present price control regulations, which existed until April 1979, an increase in the world price of oil widened the gap between imported- and domestic-oil price levels. The result of artificially low domestic prices was to reduce incentives for domestic oil production, which subsequently increased oil imports. Currently, domestic oil price controls are gradually being phased out through 1981, when all domestic oil prices will be allowed to attain world levels.[6]

An analysis of the impacts of higher imported-oil prices involves not only the increasing effects on the level of domestically produced oil but also consideration of competing–energy product prices and the probable domestic energy supply response. These responses are affected by price controls as well, especially as regards natural gas. Like oil prices, however, natural-gas prices are being deregulated gradually, beginning in April 1979.

Policy Responses

The magnitude of the impacts of any price increase on the domestic economy will depend substantially on the policy actions taken by monetary and fiscal authorities. Any such policy response will have to deal somehow with the accompanying transfer of income to foreigners, which ultimately cannot be avoided. Section V treats this subject in greater detail.

III. MODEL METHODOLOGY

Domestic Energy Price Calculations

Table 5—1 presents alternative energy price paths in levels and year-over-year rates of change for average oil import prices, domestic oil production prices, and domestic wholesale energy prices, all of which are exogenous to the model. The control set of price schedules includes the 14 percent increase in average OPEC oil prices announced at the December 1978 meeting. This implies an average annual increase of 14 percent for 1979 and 1980, but with the majority occurring in 1979. Beyond 1980, imported-oil prices are assumed to grow at an annual rate of 7 percent, which roughly yields a pattern of constant real imported-oil prices.

The three alternative oil price scenarios in this table represent calculations for world and domestic energy prices that result from (1) the announced June 1979 OPEC price schedule, (2) denominating the June 1979 schedule of prices in Special Drawing Rights (SDR) instead of dollars, and (3) the oil price schedule under assumptions of an additional 1980 increase in OPEC prices.[7] These price schedules are calculated in the same way as the control schedule, except for the difference in oil import prices.

Average domestic oil prices in the control scenario follow the schedule for decontrol of domestic oil production prices announced in April 1979. This schedule allows those prices to attain world levels by the fourth quarter of 1981. Under this decontrol plan there are four different categories of domestic oil, each with its own decontrol schedule:

1. Upper-tier oil, which accounts for over 30 percent of domestic production.[8] The price of this category will increase in equal monthly increments to adjust to the existing world oil price level, beginning in January 1980 and attaining world levels in the fourth quarter of 1981.
2. Lower-tier oil, which currently amounts to approximately 30 percent of domestic oil production, will be decontrolled toward

Table 5–1. Alternative domestic energy prices: price indices (1972 = 100) with four quarter rates of change in parentheses.

Year	Control Schedule			June 1979 OPEC Price Increase		
	Average Oil Import Prices	Domestic Oil Prices	WPI Energy	Average Oil Import Prices	Domestic Oil Prices	WPI Energy
1978 Q4	527.2	416.3	284.2	527.2	416.3	284.2
1979 Q4	666.7 (26.5)	510.6 (22.7)	333.8 (17.5)	854.8 (62.1)	583.9 (40.3)	378.5 (33.2)
1980 Q4	684.9 (2.7)	593.8 (16.3)	373.4 (11.9)	935.6 (9.5)	753.8 (29.1)	490.6 (29.6)
1981 Q4	732.8 (7.0)	732.8 (23.4)	425.5 (14.0)	1,029.1 (10.0)	1,029.1 (36.5)	588.7 (20.0)
1982 Q4	784.3 (7.0)	784.3 (7.0)	455.3 (7.0)	1,132.1 (10.0)	1,132.1 (10.0)	647.6 (10.0)
1983 Q4	839.8 (7.0)	839.8 (7.0)	487.2 (7.0)	1,245.4 (10.0)	1,245.4 (10.0)	712.4 (10.0)

the upper-tier price through a "decline rate"[9] schedule of de-controlled quantities where the rates of decontrol are 1.5 percent per month through December 1979 and 3 percent per month between January 1980 and October 1981.

3. Marginal oil, comprising mainly Alaskan North Slope and Naval Petroleum reserve oil, with a share in domestic production of less than 15 percent, four-fifths of which was raised to the upper-tier price in June 1979, with the remainder decontrolled to upper-tier prices in June 1980.

4. Noncontrolled oil, the remaining domestic category, which already sells at about the world oil price level.

With the prices of all categories of domestic oil rising in monthly increments toward world oil price levels existing in that month, an increase in imported-oil prices accelerates the increase in domestic

Table 5-1. continued

Year	June 1979 OPEC Prices in SDRs			Additional 1980 OPEC Price Increase		
	Average Oil Import Prices	Domestic Oil Prices	WPI Energy	Average Oil Import Prices	Domestic Oil Prices	WPI Energy
1978 Q4	527.2	416.3	284.2	527.3	416.3	284.2
1979 Q4	878.2 (66.6)	600.1 (44.1)	390.8 (37.5)	887.0 (68.2)	596.1 (43.2)	386.8 (36.1)
1980 Q4	972.1 (10.7)	783.1 (30.6)	509.7 (30.4)	1,138.2 (28.3)	884.5 (48.4)	575.7 (48.0)
1981 Q4	1,069.1 (10.0)	1,069.1 (36.5)	611.6 (20.0)	1,256.2 (10.4)	1,256.2 (42.0)	718.6 (24.8)
1982 Q4	1,176.1 (10.0)	1,176.1 (10.0)	672.8 (10.0)	1,381.9 (10.0)	1,381.9 (10.0)	790.5 (10.0)
1983 Q4	1,293.7 (10.0)	1,293.7 (10.0)	740.0 (10.0)	1,520.1 (10.0)	1,520.1 (10.0)	869.5 (10.0)

oil prices. This is illustrated in Figure 5-2. An upward shift in the imported-oil price path, as shown by the dotted lines, leads to a domestic price path that accelerates still more rapidly than previously, since all controls are removed by October 1, 1981. In either case, the impact on domestic oil prices is small in the early phases of decontrol and larger as price controls near expiration.

The assumptions concerning domestic wholesale energy prices take into account the direct and competing-goods price effects of higher world oil prices on domestic refined petroleum products, coal, and natural gas. To calculate the impact, we begin by converting quantities of domestic oil, coal, and natural gas produced to Btu equivalents. The Btu equivalent output shares in the three energy categories in 1972 are used to weight the impacts on the domestic wholesale energy price. The impacts are expressed in terms of percentage changes in prices in each of the three energy categories. These percentage

Figure 5–2.   The combined effect on domestic energy prices of domestic price decontrol and on external price shock.

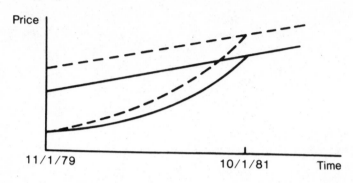

changes are calculated in two steps. First, the incremental revenue (change in price × Btu equivalent quantity) to the seller that would result from a one-dollar-per-barrel increase in OPEC prices is divided by the projected values of expenditures for each of the three categories. Next, these unadjusted incremental revenues are adjusted by an assumed domestic energy–category price response to OPEC prices.

Table 5–2 outlines the calculations for the impact of a one-dollar-increase in the OPEC price per barrel on each category of domestically produced energy.

The incremental revenues that would result from a one-dollar-per-barrel increase in OPEC prices, under the assumption that the prices of products in all three energy categories rise by the same amount, are displayed in column 1. These are adjusted by the elasticity of each category's price with respect to OPEC prices (column 2); the adjusted incremental revenues are presented in column 3.[10] In turn these are divided by a projected control level of nominal expenditures in each category to give the assumed percentage change in prices given in column 4.[11] Column 5 gives the Btu equivalent weights, and column 6 gives the percentage impacts on domestic wholesale energy prices. We adjust the wholesale energy price by the amount in the "total" row for each one-dollar-per-barrel increase in OPEC prices.

Oil Price Shocks in the MPS Model

The standard channels of transmitting the oil price shock through the MPS model structure were discussed in detail in the MPS model stud-

Table 5–2. Calculations for the impact of a one-dollar increase in OPEC price on prices of domestic energy products.

Category	(1) Unadjusted Incremental Revenue	(2) Elasticity with Respect to OPEC Prices	(3) Adjusted Incremental Revenue (1×2)	(4) Percentage of Change	(5) Weight in Btu Equivalent	(6) Effect on Domestic Wholesale Energy Prices (Percentage Increase) (4×5)
Refined petroleum products	$4.0 B	1.0	$4.00 B	5.56	0.625	3.47
Coal	1.2 B	0.2	0.24 B	1.92	0.238	0.46
Natural gas	1.7 B	0.2	0.34 B	1.07	0.137	0.15
Total					1.000	4.08

ies referred to above. The structure of the model has been modified since the publication of these studies, in part to facilitate this type of analysis. This section outlines these modifications.

The version of the MPS model used in the earlier studies was not structurally rich enough to capture all the effects of external price shocks. Consequently, in those studies such effects were modeled by judgmentally adjusting relevant model equations. The current version of the model has a disaggregated foreign sector, including current and capital accounts and an exchange-rate determination mechanism. It also has equations for all expenditure-component price deflators, which are constructed to be homogeneous with respect to the aggregate price of output. Thus, much of the structural detail necessary to simulate external price shocks is currently in the model.

Within the current account of the foreign sector,[12] the direct impact of higher world oil prices on demand is captured by the domestic petroleum demand equation. Domestic petroleum consumption (DQFL) is a function of real income (XGNP) and the exogenous wholesale price index for energy (PWIFE) relative to the implicit GNP deflator (PGNP):[13]

$$ln \text{ DQFL} = -3.8 + 0.944 \ ln \text{ XGNP} - 0.13 \ ln \text{ (PWIFE/PGNP)} \ . \tag{1}$$

The value of imports of petroleum (EMP) is then determined by an identity of the form:

$$\text{EMP} = (\text{DQFL} - \text{SQFL}) * \text{PUVFL} * k \ , \tag{2}$$

where SQFL is exogenous domestic production, PUVFL is the average import price of oil per barrel, and k is a unit conversion factor.

The MPS price sector determines a fixed weight value-added non-farm business deflator (P_{fw}) with an average markup over minimized long-run average cost specification:

$$ln \ P_{fw} = 0.2991 + 0.3039 \ ln \text{ PL} - 0.30406 \ L(7) \ ln \text{ OMH} \tag{3}$$

$$+ \ 0.0830 \ \frac{1}{U} - .0679 \ L(4) \ \Delta ln \ P_{rm}$$

$$+ \ 0.0400 \ L \ (5) \ ln \ P_f^* + 0.6962 \ ln \ P_{fw-1} \ ,$$

where L(N) is a distributed lag of N+1 quarters (including the current quarter), and where long-run minimized average cost is proxied by unit labor costs—wages (PL) divided by output per manhour

(OMH)—with a steady-state coefficient of unity. Arguments in the markup function include the inverse of the unemployment rate (U) and a foreign-exchange-rate-adjusted foreign price index relative to domestic prices (P_f^*). Raw material prices (P_{rm}) enter the equation in differenced log form. The negative coefficients reflect the fact that increases in import prices reduce a value-added deflator until the increases are fully passed through to the price of final sales.

Final-demand sector prices P_j, for $j = 1, 2, \ldots n$ expenditure categories, are estimated within a system of relative prices that consistently allocates the changes in value-added production prices throughout the system. The determinants of a typical relative-price equation include those of P_{fw}, with effects that add to zero to preserve homogeneity in P_{fw}. In addition, arguments are included to adjust the coverage from nonfarm business (that of P_{fw}) to all sectors (i.e., including farm, rest of world, and households and institutions).[14]

Additional Exogenous Assumptions

Most indirect effects of an oil price shock—wage–price interaction, contraction of real aggregate demand, the income transfer loss—are captured in the MPS model. A few of the indirect impacts, particularly on foreign income and price, are exogenous to the model.

Competing–energy product prices should have an indirect effect on the model's main price equation. However, the wholesale energy price is not included in that equation. Thus, we have calculated estimates of this effect such that a 10 percent increase in imported-energy costs raises the nonfarm business markup function by 0.7 percent.[15] This elasticity is used to apply an adjustment to the equation for P_{fw}, which in turn is automatically distributed to expenditure deflators.

Both foreign and domestic prices and activity levels enter into the model's trade and capital sector equations. We assume that the effects of higher world oil prices on U.S. trading partners will be similar to the effects on the United States. Based on other simulation experiments,[16] we assume that the elasticity of a weighted average of foreign consumption prices with respect to oil prices is 0.03.

The impact of oil price increases on foreign real activity is likely to be similar to that in the United States. However, while we can be reasonably sure of the sign, we are less sure about the magnitude of such real impacts, particularly for relatively energy-independent countries like Canada and the United Kingdom. Consequently we have ignored these real output effects. Thus, these simulation exercises do not capture a probable reduction in foreign demand for U.S. exports. The weighted average exchange rate index (taken as exogenous in this exercise) is also left unchanged, since, in our opinion, the impact of oil price changes on the exchange rate is indeterminate.

We have experimented with several alternative methods of calculating the government tax revenue and expenditure consequences of the administration's windfall profits tax proposal.[17] The net result of the proposals seemed to be a modest redistribution of nominal income from domestic oil companies to consumers, without significantly altering the multiplier results. Consequently, the simulations below ignore the windfall profits tax.

Estimates of the supply elasticity of domestically produced oil vary widely and have become more difficult to ascertain with the onset of the decontrol program. The impact of decontrol and anticipation of further increases in world oil prices is to create substantial incentives for the domestic oil production industry to delay new discovery until after 1981, when all oil prices will be decontrolled. The windfall profits tax also reduces industry incentives. Additionally, it can be assumed that discovery capacity is limited within the five-year horizon of our experiments. In view of this uncertainty, we assume there is no domestic supply response to increased world oil prices.

A variety of monetary policy assumptions can be simulated in the MPS model structure. However, the results of the simulations are virtually invariant to the specification of monetary policy because the domestic price and output effects of the oil price increase offset each other. On net, therefore, the demand for money is little changed by the shock. Consequently it makes almost no difference whether monetary aggregates, interest rates, or bank reserves are used as the exogenous policy variable in simulation.[18] Unless otherwise specified, we have held unborrowed member-bank reserves constant at levels simulated within the control simulation.

The fiscal policy assumptions in the simulations are that most nominal federal government expenditures are exogenous (so real expenditures are endogenous), and all tax rates are similarly fixed. Federal unemployment transfers and all receipts are endogenous.

Mork and Hall, in Chapter 3 of this volume, allow substitution between energy and other factor inputs in the production function that is part of their model and are able to analyze the likely effects of such substitution. The MPS model uses a two-factor production function that does not include energy and thus has no way of capturing the effect of changed energy prices on output per unit of capital and labor input. Any such effect would have to be added by assumption, and our simulations include no such adjustments. We recognize this as an area for future model development.

IV. MODEL SIMULATION RESULTS

The methodology of this exercise is standard multiplier analysis. Disturbed simulations are compared to a control simulation. The first multiplier analysis contrasts the macroeconomic responses of the model under assumptions of the announced OPEC June 1979 oil price schedule with a control simulation that employs the control schedule of energy prices in Table 5−1 above. The purpose of the second and third multiplier simulations is to highlight the continuing vulnerability of the domestic economy to further possible adverse world oil price shocks. In the second simulation, these come in the form of denominating OPEC oil prices in Special Drawing Rights rather than in dollars, assuming that this switch would have a negative impact on the confidence in the dollar. In the third simulation, the shock comes in the form of yet another OPEC price increase in 1980. We contrast the latter two simulations with the OPEC June 1979 scenario such that the multipliers represent the impacts over and above those anticipated after the June 1979 decision.

The Impacts of the June 1979 Oil Price Increase

From Table 5−1 in the preceding section we interpret the effect of the June 1979 oil price schedule as increasing average imported-oil prices in the United States by 28 percent over what they would have been by the end of 1979, and second, as increasing both imported and domestic oil by 48 percent above what they would have been by 1983. This extends the announced OPEC schedule with a 10 percent annual growth after 1979. This is higher than in the control scenario (7 percent) and takes into account higher U.S. inflation rates. The domestic wholesale price index for energy is calculated to be 34.8

percent above control levels by 1983. Table 5–3 summarizes the MPS model multiplier results.

The simulated effects of the oil price rise are quite large. Real domestic economic activity, as measured by GNP in constant 1972 dollars, is off $12.4 billion by the end of 1980 and is $48.6 billion lower by 1983 as a result of the oil price increase. The latter figure represents roughly a 3 percent decline in the level of real economic output as compared to the base projections.

The impact of the higher oil prices on domestic consumption prices, which are part of the relative price system summarized above, is to add 1.3 percent to the price level by the fourth quarter of 1980 and 2.2 percent by the end of 1983. The effects on unemployment build up gradually, with the unemployment rate increased by 1.8 percentage points by the end of the simulation, as the depressing effects of the oil price shock continue to drive domestic activity lower.

Given the large domestic price increase, it may seem surprising at first that nominal GNP is lowered relative to the control simulation. If the price increase were confined to domestically produced oil, nominal GNP would indeed be higher and real GNP lower. However, through 1981 the price increases are mostly confined to imported oil, due to the slow phasing out of domestic oil price controls. Thus, both nominal and real GNP are lower as a result of the income transfer to foreigners and the fact that the dollar increase in imports offsets the dollar increase in final sales. Hence, the early part of this exercise is dominated by the income transfer effects of higher world oil prices.

The reduction in the level of nominal GNP relative to the control simulation explains two other results. Treasury bill rates fall initially, then rise as the proportion of prices rises in (the roughly constant) nominal GNP.[19] Corporate profits also fall in absolute terms, although their share in GNP grows over time as the reduction in output more than offsets the decline in profits brought about by the higher energy prices.

The OPEC SDR-Based Pricing Scenario

The increasing size of the oil import bill in the United States balance of trade often has been cited as a continuing source of weakness in the value of the U.S. dollar. In order to avoid the erosion of its

Table 5–3. Effect of increased oil price projections (difference from control simulation).

	1979		1980				1981				1982	1983
	3	4	1	2	3	4	1	2	3	4	4	4
Nominal GNP ($bill)	-3.5	-6.4	-4.5	-3.0	-2.5	-2.6	-3.0	-3.4	-3.6	-6.2	-24.5	-53.8
Real GNP ($bill 1972)	-3.0	-5.8	-6.1	-8.1	-10.1	-12.4	-15.0	-18.1	-21.4	-24.9	-37.8	-48.6
GNP deflator (percent)	0.1	0.1	0.3	0.5	0.6	0.8	1.0	1.2	1.4	1.5	1.8	1.5
Consumption deflator (percent)	0.4	0.6	0.7	0.9	1.1	1.3	1.4	1.7	1.9	2.1	2.4	2.2
Unemployment rate (percentage points)	0.0	0.1	0.2	0.2	0.3	0.4	0.5	0.6	0.7	0.8	1.4	1.8
Treasury bill rate (percentage points)	-0.0	-0.0	0.0	0.1	0.1	0.1	0.1	0.1	0.1	0.1	0.0	-0.1
Net exports ($bill)	-8.8	-12.1	-9.4	-9.1	-8.9	-9.1	-8.3	-7.5	-6.8	-7.1	-8.8	-10.7
Corporate profits ($bill)	-3.5	-5.6	-3.3	-1.7	-1.0	-0.8	-0.0	0.9	2.6	2.4	0.1	-1.6

dollar-denominated income, OPEC may choose in the future to tie its price to a basket of currencies, such as the Special Drawing Rights (SDR) of the International Monetary Fund. Such a decision would, in our view, portend a loss of confidence—at least in the short run—in the value of the dollar as a medium of exchange for a major item of world trade, and would probably contribute to its decline.

Our interest in this exercise is the passthrough of exchange rate changes to U.S. oil import prices under such an OPEC pricing system. We arbitrarily assume a 10 percent depreciation of the dollar on a multilateral trade-weighted basis as a result of this change and calculate its resultant impact on the dollar price per barrel of oil imported into the United States. We approximate such a scenario by first shocking the model's endogenous exchange rate–determining process sufficiently to cause a gradual 10 percent depreciation of the dollar exchange rate index. Feedbacks from the rest of the model on the exchange rate attenuate the depreciation as the trade balance improves.[20]

The U.S. dollar represents approximately one-third of a multilateral trade-weighted SDR exchange rate index. Hence, an average dollar depreciation of 10 percent will roughly increase the average value of the SDR index by 6 2/3 percent. If there is no further change in SDR-based OPEC prices, this would eventually add one dollar to the cost of an average imported-oil barrel for U.S residents above the June 1979 OPEC dollar-based price. In Table 5–4 we contrast the additional macroeconomic effects of this assumption with those incorporated in the scenario of the June 1979 OPEC price increase.

By the end of the simulation period, real GNP is $10 billion (1972) lower, the consumption price level is increased 2 percent, and the unemployment rate is 0.4 percentage points higher than in the June 1979 scenario. This comes as a result of the exchange rate depreciation and its SDR-based passthrough to oil import prices. Exchange rate impact simulations we have performed with the MPS model (see Hooper and Lowrey 1979) indicate that, of the combined exchange rate–OPEC SDR oil price simulation effects in this scenario, the induced oil price increase effects account for a $12 billion decline in real GNP, a 0.5 percent increase in the level of consumption prices, and most of the rise in the unemployment rate.

The multiplier difference between these two experiments involves the usual effects of a decline in the value of the dollar, together with the induced exchange rate increase in the dollar price per barrel of

Table 5–4. Effect of OPEC oil prices linked to SDR basket of currencies (*difference from June 1979 OPEC simulation*).

	1979		1980				1981				1982	1983
	3	4	1	2	3	4	1	2	3	4	4	4
Nominal GNP ($bill)	5.3	7.5	12.7	18.5	24.0	27.5	28.5	27.8	28.2	31.1	35.0	38.0
Real GNP ($bill 1972)	−0.9	−1.4	−1.1	−0.9	−0.8	−1.2	−2.3	−3.8	−4.7	−4.7	−7.0	−10.0
GNP deflator (percent)	−0.0	0.2	0.3	0.5	0.7	0.8	1.0	1.0	1.1	1.2	1.5	1.8
Consumption deflator (percent)	0.4	0.5	0.6	0.8	0.9	1.0	1.1	1.2	1.3	1.4	1.8	2.0
Unemployment rate (percentage points)	0.0	0.0	0.0	0.0	0.0	0.0	0.1	0.1	0.2	0.2	0.3	0.4
Treasury bill rate (percentage points)	0.0	0.0	0.0	0.0	0.0	0.0	0.0	0.0	0.0	0.0	0.0	0.0
Net exports ($bill)	0.2	0.6	3.1	5.8	8.1	8.9	7.9	6.5	6.0	7.2	7.1	7.2
Corporate profits ($bill)	4.6	6.3	9.7	12.9	15.6	16.7	16.1	14.9	15.1	17.3	20.0	23.0
Exchange rate (percent)	−3.8	−8.5	−9.1	−9.2	−9.3	−8.8	−7.7	−6.3	−7.7	−9.0	−9.5	−9.4
Import oil price ($ per barrel)	0.18	0.59	0.85	0.88	0.90	0.92	0.94	1.00	1.00	1.00	1.00	1.00

imported oil. The exchange rate impact on the economy has a longer lag than does that of an oil price increase. This is due in part to the price lags in the nonoil trade equations, and in part to the lags in transmitting exchange rate changes into prices. Thus, a depreciation of the dollar alone would *increase* real GNP as the trade balance improved (although eventually these effects would be offset by the increase in the price level), whereas in the present case, GNP is reduced. A depreciation of the dollar increases both output and the price level, unlike an oil price increase alone, so this scenario is not insensitive to the monetary policy instrument. We highlight this sensitivity in this scenario by holding the Treasury bill rate fixed at rates derived from the June 1979 OPEC oil price simulation from which the present exercise multipliers are calculated. This gives an extreme impression of the inflationary and output effects, since this monetary policy option of the model accommodates all of the rise in income and prices.

Additional OPEC Price Increase Scenario

In the first scenario, world oil price levels beyond the schedule announced by OPEC in June 1979 were projected to grow at a nominal 10 percent annual rate. This extension is based on an assumed desire by OPEC to keep real prices roughly constant after the large 1979 increase, as was the case after 1974. Recent events suggest, however, that this assumption is optimistic.[21]

Hence, we postulate further discrete OPEC price increases and assume the worse case—that they come quickly. In this experiment we add an additional world oil price increase, beginning in the third quarter of 1979, which raises imported-oil prices 21.7 percent by the fourth quarter of 1980 above those assumed in the June 1979 scenario. By the end of 1980, domestic oil production prices are 17.3 percent higher than the June 1979 scenario levels, as they adjust more rapidly to catch up to world price levels. By the end of 1983, both domestic and world oil prices attain levels 22.1 percent higher than the June 1979 scenario prices. Domestic wholesale energy prices, which include competing energy prices of coal and natural gas, are about 20 percent higher by the fourth quarter of 1983 than those assumed in the June 1979 OPEC scenario.

Here again we contrast the simulated effects of this experiment with those of the June 1979 scenario. Table 5–5 summarizes the

Table 5–5. Effect of additional OPEC price increases in 1980 (*difference from OPEC June 1979 scenario*).

	1979		1980				1981				1982	1983
	3	4	1	2	3	4	1	2	3	4	4	4
Nominal GNP ($bill)	-0.6	-1.0	-1.9	-2.4	-0.9	0.5	1.3	1.6	1.7	-0.3	-12.0	-26.0
Real GNP ($bill 1972)	-0.5	-0.9	-3.5	-5.9	-7.0	-8.3	-9.9	-11.9	-14.3	-17.0	-26.1	-32.6
GNP deflator (percent)	0.0	0.0	0.2	0.3	0.4	0.6	0.7	0.9	1.1	1.2	1.4	1.4
Consumption deflator (percent)	0.1	0.1	0.5	0.7	0.8	1.0	1.2	1.3	1.5	1.6	1.8	1.8
Unemployment rate (percentage points)	0.0	0.0	0.1	0.1	0.2	0.3	0.3	0.4	0.5	0.6	1.0	1.3
Treasury bill rate (percentage points)	-0.0	-0.0	-0.0	0.0	0.0	0.1	0.1	0.1	0.1	0.1	0.1	-0.0
Net exports ($bill)	-1.4	-1.9	-7.6	-9.4	-7.7	-6.6	-5.8	-5.0	-4.3	-4.2	-4.5	-5.3
Corporate profits ($bill)	-0.6	-0.9	-2.0	-2.1	-0.5	1.0	2.0	2.6	3.4	2.9	1.1	1.6

multiplier results. These results indicate an additional $32.6 billion (1972) reduction in real GNP, a 1.8 percent increase in consumption price levels, and a further 1.3 percentage point increase in the unemployment rate by the end of the simulation period as a result of the further oil price increase.

V. POLICY RESPONSES TO THE OIL PRICE INCREASE

It is likely that policy authorities would attempt to offset recessionary and inflationary impacts of oil price increases such as those reported above. In this section we briefly outline some anticipated problems with policy responses to the effects of oil price shocks in the context of the MPS model multiplier results.

Fiscal policy can do much in the short run to offset the income transfer to OPEC countries, provided that monetary policy is accommodating and provided that the OPEC countries are willing to hold U.S. government debt. Suppose that OPEC buys *no* U.S. goods with the incremental revenue it obtains by raising oil prices. Instead, it is willing to hold financial claims on the United States. Further suppose that the fiscal authorities cut taxes so as to exactly restore the income lost through the oil price–induced transfer. The increased government deficit must be financed, say by issuing securities. If, even indirectly, OPEC buys all the government securities issued, the fiscal authorities have passed the income effects of the oil price increase on to future generations—the current costs being interest on the debt.[22]

However, the price level is still increased, so the stance of monetary policy is crucially important to the effects of the fiscal offset. Even though foreign residents are holding the increase in public debt (so that the new government securities are not competing with, and crowding out, private debt in capital markets), nonaccomodating monetary policy would result in higher interest rates and eventually no real effect of the fiscal action—complete crowding out. If, however, the monetary authority were willing to tolerate the increase in the price level, the fiscal action would effectively pass on to future generations the costs of the oil price increase. Hence, the choice for policymakers is whether to pay now or later.

Suppose, however, that OPEC does buy goods and services from the United States with the revenues generated by the oil price increase. In this case, there is no way—even in the short run—to avoid that part of the real income transfer associated with the decline in U.S. terms of trade; that is, the United States must give up more real resources to import a barrel of oil. It is true that the aggregate demand loss will be partially offset by the increase in U.S. exports. However, this demand offset will not reduce the loss in real income.

Tax policy can have microeconomic effects by changing relative prices, perhaps to offset the effects of an oil price rise. If energy, capital, and labor are all substitutes in production, an oil price increase, like a tax on energy, lowers the prices of capital and labor relative to energy, and producers will shift toward more labor- and capital-intensive technologies.

Unfortunately, energy is probably complementary to the capital equipment it powers, so an increase in energy prices lowers the factor demand for both capital and energy. Tax policy designed to stimulate investment as a response to an oil price rise will lower the cost of capital. In the short run, investment embodying new technology that is more energy-saving will likely be made, resulting in increases in both actual and potential ouput. However, the revenue loss to the Treasury from the tax cuts must be financed somehow. If it is financed by raising other taxes, the short-run increases in output will likely be offset by reductions in aggregate demand. If it is financed by borrowing, the increased investment will eventually be crowded out by the reduction in government savings, unless OPEC is again willing to undertake the increase in savings required to finance the increase in investment.

In both the short and longer runs, there can be no increase in aggregate investment without an increase in aggregate savings. This fundamental principle of economics is frequently overlooked in discussing the effects of tax policy on investment. It may be that a cut in personal taxes, particularly capital gains taxes, and elimination of the double taxation of dividends, would elicit more saving. However, the empirical and theoretical evidence on this is mixed.[23]

There is no one "correct" monetary policy response to the effects of the increased world oil prices. The monetary authorities can respond in two opposite directions: Either they can accommodate the inflationary impulse or they can attempt to offset the resulting increase in prices. In the Pierce–Enzler analysis of external sources of domestic inflation, the monetary response to such a shock was dubbed a "slippery" concept at best (Pierce and Enzler 1974). The direction of monetary policy response rests on the specification of the policymaker's objective function, which must include, inter alia, paths of both expected inflation and unemployment over time. The nature of the short-term external inflationary impulse is such that no choice of monetary policy can lead to the unambiguously better situation of lower paths for both inflation and unemployment. The policy dilemma is even more unattractive due to the current situation of both high inflation and slow real growth. The important fact is that, as with fiscal policy, monetary policy faces a pay-now-or-pay-later situation—in the long run it cannot offset the income transfer to OPEC.

In the multiplier experiments analyzed in this paper, we have made no extraordinary assumptions concerning the response of fiscal or monetary policy to the oil price shocks within the context of the MPS model. In the period between the first and final drafts of this paper, the projected pattern of world oil prices has evolved toward the "additional OPEC price increase scenario," with the stance of both fiscal and monetary policy substantially less accommodating than assumed in these simulations. These developments, and their potential impacts as suggested in the multipliers above, highlight the continuing vulnerability of the U.S. economy to world oil price shocks. This paper's analysis of this vulnerability does not propose a "best" policy response to these shocks. The concluding observations on policy alternatives above demonstrate that all the policy choices are difficult and each choice has its own set of economic costs.

NOTES TO CHAPTER 5

1. The results of these studies are broadly consistent with the empirical studies by Eckstein (1978), Klein (1978), Mork and Hall (1980b), and Perry (1975b).

2. Price controls for domestic oil are assumed to be fully effective. This differs from the assumptions in Chapter 3.

3. The weights for average import prices are import share weights, and for domestic oil prices, production weights, obtained from various issues of *Monthly Energy Review*. Btu-equivalent output weights for the domestic wholesale energy price index from the *Survey of Current Business* are also calculated from this source.

4. Cf. Berner et al. (1975).

5. The unique characteristics of world oil price increases as they affect world-wide inflation are discussed in Salant (1977).

6. The proposed domestic production oil price decontrol plan is described in Office of the White House Press Secretary (1979), "The White House Fact Sheet."

7. At the time this analysis was carried out, this scenario was viewed as pessimistic. Out of the three scenarios, this corresponds most closely to the actual experience of late 1979 and early 1980.

8. Since the analysis done for this paper was completed, these percentages have changed substantially as a result of the decontrol program.

9. By "decline rate" is meant that each month a fraction of production will be allowed to sell at the upper-tier price.

10. The elasticity for domestic refined petroleum product prices rises to 1.0 by the fourth quarter of 1981 when all controls are gone. For prior quarters, the elasticity is a weighted average of the response in each of the four petroleum categories described above and is based on the decontrol assumptions.

11. Real quantities are assumed constant in these calculations, according to the low short-run energy elasticities assumed throughout this analysis. While these assumptions make the calculated percentage changes an upper bound on the competing goods energy price impact, it is our belief that the majority of the impact of imported oil price shocks are evidenced in price responses with little or no output responses.

12. See Thurman (1977a).

13. The absence of lags in the equation, especially for the relative price term, means that the impact on demand probably is underscored, since the long-run elasticity is likely to be larger than 0.13.

14. The relative price system for final expenditure prices is explained in Thurman (1977b, 1979).

15. This calculation is derived as the sum of adjusted incremental revenues in column 3 of Table 5-2 divided by a projected base path for nominal nonfarm business output. The actual adjustment varies with the decontrol assumptions. The assumption is again made that quantities are unchanged.

16. These experiments include those simulated with the Federal Reserve Board's multicountry model (Berner et al. forthcoming), a modified version of the MPS model (Thurman 1979), and an EEC trade model (Berner 1976).

17. At the time the underlying research was carried out, the final form of this tax was not known.

18. For this reason the correction to the money demand function made by Pierce and Enzler (1974) is not made here.

19. The elasticity of money demand in the MPS model is one with respect to prices but less than one with respect to real output, so with respect

to nominal GNP, the elasticity depends on the mix of output and price changes.

20. For a theoretical description of the MPS model exchange rate determination, see Urdang (1979). The importance of feedback effects is discussed in Hooper and Lowrey (1979).

21. The reader should be reminded that the world oil prices of late 1979 and early 1980 were unknown at the time this research was carried out.

22. Assuming it is either short-term debt that is rolled over or long-term coupon debt.

23. For a thorough discussion of this issue, see Von Furstenberg and Malkiel (1977).

6 AN ECONOMIC ANALYSIS OF PETROLEUM IMPORT REDUCTION POLICIES
Energy Conservation versus New Supply*

*Richard J. Goettle IV**

I. INTRODUCTION

Recent developments affecting the price, availability, and safety of conventional energy supplies have led to renewed concern over current domestic energy policy and have provided an opportunity to define and clarify its direction. In the process of review, it is important to compare and evaluate alternative policy strategies to ensure that the chosen strategy yields the best combination of benefits relative to the costs incurred. The analysis of this chapter is a contribution to the review of energy policy options.

Three major strategies are considered as possible directions for future energy policy. The first is to introduce no new policies be-

*The analysis underlying this chapter was sponsored by the Office of Policy, Planning, and Evaluation under the Assistant Secretary for Conservation and Solar Energy, U.S. Department of Energy. Neither the United States nor the United States Department of Energy, nor any of their employees, nor any of their contractors, subcontractors, or their employees, makes any warranty, express or implied, or assumes any legal liability or responsibility for the accuracy, completeness, or usefulness of any information, apparatus, product, or process disclosed, or represents that its use would not infringe upon privately owned rights.

**Senior Economist, Dale W. Jorgenson Associates. Numerous individuals were involved in the analytical effort from which this paper was developed. The principals included Edward A. Hudson and this author from Dale W. Jorgenson Associates, and Harry Davitian, Paul J. Groncki, Peter Kleeman, and Joan Lukachinski from Brookhaven National Laboratory.

yond those presently in effect. The second strategy involves a redirection of policy toward energy conservation. The third strategic option is to promote increased domestic supply, primarily through an accelerated commercial development of the so-called synthetic and unconventional fuels.

The consequences of these policy alternatives are examined for the period 1980 to 2000, using the combined Brookhaven National Laboratory/Dale W. Jorgenson Associates (BNL/DJA) energy-economy model system (Lukachinski et al. 1979). The DJA economic model (LITM) depicts production and spending throughout the economy within a flexible interindustry framework (Hudson and Jorgenson 1977). The model provides for substitutions in the final spending on the goods and services that constitute the Gross National Product (GNP). Further, it permits substitution in each producing sector among the capital, labor, energy, and materials inputs to production. The BNL component of the system (TESOM) is a technological model of energy extraction, conversion, and end use (Kydes and Rabinowitz 1979). It represents the economic, technical, and environmental characteristics of the future substitution possibilities among new and conventional energy technologies and energy sources. The combined models give a comprehensive long-run representation of the nation's energy and economic systems, energy-economy interactions, and the environmental consequences of these. Using this integrated system, the method of analysis is, first, to project developments under the no-new-policy strategy and, then, to perform alternative projections corresponding to each of the more active policies. The three cases are then compared in order to estimate:

1. The relative merits of the strategies with respect to national energy security objectives
2. The costs and benefits to the U.S. economy for each strategy
3. The environmental consequences arising from the energy system under each strategy

Focusing on the economic results, the purpose of this chapter is to report the major findings of this comparison and, from these, to develop implications for the future direction of national energy policy.[1]

II. ASSUMPTIONS AND METHODOLOGY

The Reference Projection—No New Policy

The LITM economic model requires input assumptions on future population, government expenditure and revenue policies, and the unemployment rate. The Census Bureau's Series II population projections (fertility rate of 2.1) were used to derive figures on the future population. Labor force participation rates are endogenous to the model and are not specified as assumptions. The unemployment rate is assumed to follow a cyclical rate from 6.0 percent in 1978 to 5.6 percent in 1985, then to decline slightly over the rest of the forecast period. Government purchases increase slightly, relative to the rest of the economy (from 19.4 percent of real GNP in 1980 to 19.9 percent by 2000), reflecting current trends of government programs, including new developments in the areas of welfare services, energy, and defense. Government transfers and tax revenues rise approximately in line with the economy as a whole. Differential sectoral, and, hence, aggregate, productivity effects in the model are, for the most part, endogenous, while the energy supply and energy productivity information is obtained from the TESOM model. This feature of the combined model system is both a major determinant of, and an important explanation for, the nature and magnitude of energy-economy interactions.

The reference projection incorporates a variety of energy system assumptions: prices and availabilities of energy resources; capital and operating costs for electricity generation, synthetic fuel production, and end-use devices; market penetration rates for new energy technologies; and changes in efficiencies of fuel conversion over the 1980 to 2000 time horizon. The energy assumptions include the impacts of policy initiatives or actions already legislated or already announced and under control of the executive branch. In particular, the oil import quotas announced by President Carter in his energy initiatives speech of July 15, 1979 are incorporated.[2] These quotas require that future annual levels of oil imports never exceed the 1977 level, and that they be reduced to one-half the 1977 level by 1990.

Domestic pricing assumptions are based on the phased decontrol of domestic oil prices by the year 1981. A windfall profits tax (proposed, but not enacted at the time of analysis) is not included. The National Energy Plan (NEP) II High Price Trajectory is assumed for world oil prices (U.S. Department of Energy 1979a). This has the real price of oil in the world market rising at an average annual rate of 3.3 percent, from $20 per barrel in 1980 to $38 by the year 2000 (in 1978 dollars). Domestic natural-gas prices are assumed to be deregulated by 1985 and then to increase rapidly, approaching the crude-oil price; this takes the price from $0.99 per million Btu to $5.50 by the year 2000.

Domestic oil and gas production possibilities are determined by applying a Hubbert Curve analysis to the U.S. Geological Survey mean geology estimates of January 1, 1978 (U.S. Department of Energy 1979b). Nuclear electric generating capacity is assumed to reach 155 gigawatts during the 1985 to 1990 period, and to increase to a range of 225 to 240 gigawatts by the year 2000.

A set of measures of environmental effects is generated from each TESOM solution, using emission and conversion factors associated with each activity. The impacts measured include air contaminants, water contaminants, solid waste materials, and items such as radiation exposure levels and occupational injuries. The emission and conversion factors assume that best available control technologies are used in each process in the system, and that the effectiveness of these control technologies does not change over time.

The BNL/TESOM and DJA/LITM models are coupled, so in each year there is a consistency between the energy and economic information obtainable from each model. This coupling is achieved through an iterative process in which the principal points of interaction are:

1. The economic activities of each sector and the aggregate energy inputs to the producing sectors, household sectors, and other final demands;
2. The relationship between the aggregate energy inputs to the producing and consuming sectors and the levels of the nonsubstitutable, functional energy services;
3. The details of energy prices, technology production functions, quantities, imports, and the levels of new and conventional energy technologies;
4. The relationship among the energy sector details, aggregate energy and nonenergy input substitutions, product substitutions and compositional changes in final demand, and the growth of the economy from both demand and supply points of view.

The two models interface at the point of energy demand, with LITM linking aggregate energy demand to the general economy and with TESOM linking primary resources to energy demand. The linked system extends the coverage and applicability of each model and provides a framework for the consistent analysis of the role of energy technologies, energy supply and conversion and their environmental consequences, energy-economy interactions, and economic effects.

The Conservation Projection

Beginning with Fiscal Year 1981 (FY 1981), the conservation policy is represented by the additional energy savings and the associated incremental expenditures, public and private alike, arising from a set of conservation initiatives from the Office of Assistant Secretary for Conservation and Solar Energy (CSE). The expenditure and energy information is provided by material prepared by CSE personnel (U.S. Department of Energy 1978). As the energy savings and costs for these initiatives are over and above those envisioned in the no-new-policy situation, a projection developed with these programs in place affords, by comparison, the direct determination of the energy, economic, and environmental consequences of the demand-reduction strategy.

The conservation policy, as described in the CSE materials, incorporates subprograms into major program areas as follows:

1. Buildings and community systems
2. Transportation
3. Industrial
4. State and local programs
5. Appropriate technology

The supporting documentation for the conservation policy contains information for each subprogram as to the direct benefits and costs of the particular initiative. The direct policy benefits are represented by the levels of annual energy savings (1985, 1990, and 2000); the direct costs are reflected in the cumulative public and private expenditures, discounted to the present (FY 1981), that are required to achieve the ultimate levels of energy savings.

The energy displacements induced by the CSE programs are analyzed as demand reductions from the levels projected for the no-new-policy situation. These energy reductions permit the annual release of those resources associated with production and/or importation of petroleum, natural gas, and electricity. However, these benefits are not costless. They result from a temporally phased diversion of productive resources, public and private alike, into those activities implied for each of the conservation initiatives. The annual benefits from conservation policy are measured against the annual claims on the inputs available to the economy. These claims are implicit in the CSE discounted expenditure information and are represented by a reallocation of capital and labor services from other productive uses to energy conservation activities.

The total cost information for each subprogram, shown in Table 6-1, results from the discounting of an annual series of expenditures. In order to determine the capital and labor services claims due to this policy, it is necessary to:

1. Develop the annual expenditures series for each subprogram
2. Allocate annual expenditures between investment purchases and labor services expenditures
3. Convert the investment expenditures series into a capital services series

Rules that are specific to each subprogram are required for converting the total discounted costs into an undiscounted expenditure stream. Three types of distribution mechanisms are used to annualize and undiscount the total cost. These are denoted the uniform, constant-rate-of-growth, and trapezoidal distribution patterns.

The uniform distribution assumes constant annual expenditures for the duration of the program. It is chosen for subprograms in which all costs are incurred in the first year and those that require a series of constant annual expenditures for some number of years. The costs for these subprograms have virtually no private-sector content and, hence, the uniform distribution conforms closely to the public-outlay patterns reported in the CSE documentation.

In subprograms where initial costs of research, development, and demonstration (R, D, and D) are followed by costs that grow in proportion to annual energy savings, a constant-rate-of-growth distribution is the appropriate rule. The growth rates for these distributions are determined from the growth of energy savings over the period 1980-2000, with an allowance for economies of scale—that is, the

Table 6–1.   Total discounted costs: conservation policy.

Program	Discounted Public and Private Cost (Millions of 1972 Dollars)	
Buildings/Community systems		55,857
Buildings systems	20,271	
Appliance standards	5,619	
Community systems	5,152	
Urban waste	6,264	
Technology and consumer products	4,401	
Analysis and technology transfer	6,343	
Residential conservation service	2,711	
Federal energy management program	4,453	
Small business	643	
Transportation		40,074
Vehicle propulsion RD&D	13,681	
Electric vehicle RD&D	3,940	
Transportation system utilization	4,495	
Alternative fuels utilization	17,958	
Industrial		14,798
Waste energy reduction	5,299	
Industrial cogeneration	6,243	
Industrial process efficiency	3,253	
Implementation and deployment	3	
State and local		471
Schools and hospitals	6	
Local government buildings	0.1	
Weatherization assistance	409	
Energy management partnership act	56	
Appropriate technology		4,554
Small-scale technology	4,554	

diminution of cost per million Btu, resulting from increased market penetrations.

The trapezoidal distribution is selected for subprograms that initially require increasing R, D, and D expenditures that level off for some length of time as the product or service provided by the program increases its penetration or effectiveness, or nears commercialization. These periods are followed by a period of decreasing unit costs resulting from the influences of increased market penetration and information diffusion. In essence, this distribution mechanism is applicable to subprograms for which the most likely expenditure pattern is concentrated toward the earlier years.

The annual expenditures associated with each subprogram are next divided into investment and labor services purchases in accordance with the type of expenditure implied by the success of that subprogram. Thus, the allocation between investment and labor is determined from the corresponding expenditure shares of the total sectoral output most closely resembling the purchases implied for a successful CSE program. The information for this allocation is provided by "The Input–Output Structure of the U.S. Economy, 1972," as reported in the February 1979 *Survey of Current Business*.

Finally, the stream of annual investment expenditures for each subprogram is converted into a capital services series that reflects the permanency of the services available from the undepreciated capital stock.

The resulting series for capital and labor services represent the annual resource claims—that is, the direct policy costs—associated with the annual energy savings provided by each of the CSE initiatives. For the years 1990 and 2000, summaries of the costs and energy savings are provided, by major program area, in Table 6–2.

In the BNL energy model, conservation is represented as a new source of the delivered energy required to satisfy particular end uses, for example, space heat, process heat, motive power, and so forth. Conservation in the CSE documentation is specified as primary energy savings in the residential, commercial, industrial, and transportation sectors. The primary energy savings in each program area are allocated to specific end uses in accordance with the relative importance of the end use in the consuming sector to which the conservation subprograms are directed. Then, for each end use, the delivered-energy inputs in the reference projection are converted to their primary energy equivalents and an average conversion efficiency

Table 6-2. Assumed annual costs and energy savings: conservation policy.

Year	Major Program	Annual Resource Claims (Costs) (Millions of 1972 Dollars)			Energy Savings (Quadrillion Btu)
		Capital	Labor	Total	
1990	Buildings/Community systems	2,506	5,078	7,584	5.600
	Transportation	971	3,001	3,972	1.894
	Industrial	645	1,319	1,964	2.520
	State and local	12	0	12	0.005
	Appropriate technology	247	392	639	0.250
	Total	4,381	9,790	14,171	10.269
2000	Buildings/Community systems	3,216	2,884	6,100	10.000
	Transportation	4,457	12,074	16,531	7.372
	Industrial	634	460	1,094	4.250
	State and local	5	0	5	0.005
	Appropriate technology	283	152	435	0.630
	Total	8,595	15,570	24,165	22.257

(delivered Btu per Btu of primary energy) is determined. This, when multiplied by the primary energy savings in each end-use category, determines the delivered-energy savings resulting from conservation activities. For each end-use demand, a constraint is introduced into the energy model. These constraints restrict total delivered-energy inputs to a particular end use to be no greater than the total from the reference projection less the delivered-energy savings as determined above.

The Synthetic and Unconventional Fuels Projection

The synfuels policy is represented by the program proposed by President Carter on July 15, 1979.[3] This program provides for the accelerated commercial development of synthetic and unconventional fuels. The policy objective is stated as an incremental production target of 2.5 million barrels (crude-oil equivalent) daily from these technologies by the year 1990. The allocation of this increment, in millions of barrels per day (mmbd), is: coal liquefaction and coal methanol, 1.25 mmbd; high-Btu coal gas, 0.25 mmbd; shale oil, 0.40 mmbd; biomass, 0.10 mmbd; unconventional gas (tight sand formations, Devonian shales, coal bed, and geopressurized methane), 0.50 mmbd. Reflecting this acceleration, growth in the output of these fuels is projected to continue over the post–1990 period. This growth occurs at a more moderate rate than that in the reference projection, though it originates from a significantly higher 1990 base. The annual incremental costs and production amounts for the synfuels policy are presented in Table 6–3.

The synfuels policy is introduced into the model system in the following manner. Constraints, establishing minimum production levels for the outputs of the synfuels technologies, are incorporated into the TESOM model. In effect, these override the competitive behavior of synfuels (as evidenced in the market penetrations of the reference projection and determined by the TESOM solution algorithm). From here, the combined model system is iterated as usual.

Table 6–3. Assumed annual, incremental costs and energy production: synfuels policy.

Year	Technology	Annual, Incremental Cost (Billions of 1972 Dollars)	Incremental Production (Quadrillion Btu)
1990	Coal liquids/Methanol	7.4	2.3
	High-Btu coal gas	1.3	0.5
	Shale oil	3.2	0.8
	Biomass	0.6	0.2
	Unconventional gas	4.2	1.1
	Total	16.7	4.9
2000	Coal liquids/Methanol	16.6	4.5
	High-Btu coal gas	2.7	0.9
	Shale oil	11.1	2.1
	Biomass	0.8	0.2
	Unconventional gas	5.8	1.1
	Total	37.0	8.8

III. THE ECONOMIC EFFECTS OF ALTERNATIVE ENERGY POLICIES

Introducing policies to encourage the curtailment of the growth in energy demand or to promote the accelerated expansion of domestic energy supply has a significant effect on the growth and structure of the nation's economy. In general, the conservation policy is economically superior to the synfuels policy in achieving energy reductions consistent with national objectives. However, each policy incurs a higher economic cost than the alternative of no new policy.

Comparative final output and productivity measures for the policy alternatives are shown in Table 6–4. Through 1990, both policies yield slower growth in real GNP than the reference projection. In the

Table 6–4. Output and productivity.

	Reference	Conservation	Synfuels
1990			
Real GNP	1,901.3	1,899.1	1,888.9
Real GNP per capita	7.808	7.799	7.757
Gross labor productivity	16.885	16.881	16.805
2000			
Real GNP	2,469.3	2,473.7	2,413.3
Real GNP per capita	9.483	9.500	9.268
Gross labor productivity	19.834	19.869	19.462
Average Annual Growth Rates			
1980–1990			
Real GNP	2.98	2.97	2.92
Real GNP per capita	2.04	2.03	1.98
Gross labor productivity	1.54	1.54	1.49
1990–2000			
Real GNP	2.65	2.68	2.48
Real GNP per capita	1.96	1.99	1.80
Gross labor productivity	1.62	1.64	1.48

Note: Real GNP is in units of billions of 1972 dollars.
Real GNP per capita is in units of thousands of 1972 dollars per person.
Gross labor productivity is in units of thousands of 1972 dollars per worker.

case of conservation, the reduction in output is $2.2 billion (1972), or 0.1 percent. This policy, to be successful, requires significant commitments of the capital and labor resources available within the economy. These additional claims are measured against the release of resources permitted by conservation—that is, reductions in the required levels of energy production. To the extent that resource claims exceed releases, additional resources must be diverted from other productive uses because of their strictly limited availabilities. This reallocation is not costless in terms of economic efficiency.

For the synfuels policy, the causes of the $12.4 billion (1972) reduction in the 1990 level of real GNP are similar. Expanding domestic supply by means of synthetic and unconventional fuels requires the deployment of technologies that provide energy at a cost not yet competitive with the energy from the conventional sources they displace. As there is a substantial drain on the resources available for other productive activities, the synfuels policy imposes a significant cost in terms of income and production foregone. This cost is greater than that caused by the conservation policy and, consequently, has a more permanent effect on future economic performance.

By the year 2000, the synfuels policy is projected to result in additional economic penalties. Even though the synfuels technologies have become increasingly more competitive with conventional energy supplies, their accelerated commercial deployment has had a cumulative, adverse impact of sufficient magnitude to preclude economic recovery. In 2000, the level of real GNP under the synfuels policy is 2.3 percent, or $56.0 billion (1972) below that in the reference projection.

However, the conservation policy provides net economic benefits in this period. Here, the total resource claims of the conservation activities are more than equally compensated by the benefits of energy displacements and reduced energy production. The gains in economic efficiency from providing lower cost energy through conservation permit an increase in the net output. That is, real GNP is increased to $2,473.7 billion (1972), 0.2 percent above the reference case level.

With annual rates of labor force expansion approximately equal for the three cases, the macroeconomic impacts of the alternative policies translate directly into productivity effects. For the period 1980 to 1990, the rates of advance in gross labor productivity for the

Table 6–5.   Energy and economic growth.

Year	Policy	Real GNP (Billions of 1972 Dollars)	Primary Energy (Quadrillion Btu)	Energy-GNP Ratio (Thousand Btu per 1972 Dollar)
1990	Reference	1,901.3	96.9	51.0
	Conservation	1,899.1	86.6	45.6
	Synfuels	1,888.9	98.9	52.4
2000	Reference	2,469.3	109.5	44.3
	Conservation	2,473.7	87.2	35.3
	Synfuels	2,813.3	112.4	46.6

reference and conservation projections are almost identical. More-over, they lie above the rate resulting under synfuels policy. To the end of the century, the productivity advance associated with conservation dominates those of the other cases.

The implications for the aggregate economic efficiency of energy use under these policies are quite clear. The energy–GNP ratio and its components are shown in Table 6–5. Conservation provides a dramatic acceleration of the gains realized for this measure over the projection horizon. Conversely, the synfuels policy slows the rate of improvement relative to the reference case. For conservation, the annual rate of decline in the energy–GNP ratio is 2.4 percent for the period 1980 to 1990 and 2.5 percent to the year 2000. These are slightly more and less than double the rates of improvement observed for the synfuels and reference projections, respectively.

The changes in the pattern of economic growth are illustrated further by the division of total final output into consumption and investment purchases. These are presented in Table 6–6. In 1990, consumption absorbs 89 percent of the decline in real GNP under the synfuels policy. Investment accounts for the remaining 11 percent of the GNP decline. In 2000, under this policy, the fractions of the total decline in real economic activity attributable to consumption and investment are 85 and 15 percent, respectively. The losses in overall economic efficiency due to the synfuels policy reduce the net output and corresponding incomes that are achievable within the economy. In the static sense, investment, as a component of aggregate demand, is reduced because of the reduction in real income and the associated decline in saving. In each year that investment falls,

Table 6–6.   Economic output and expenditure.

		Reference	Conservation	Synfuels
Real GNP components (billions of 1972 dollars)				
1990	Consumption	1,235.2	1,233.1	1,224.2
	Investment	283.7	283.6	282.3
	GNP	1,901.3	1,899.1	1,888.9
2000	Consumption	1,605.6	1,607.7	1,557.8
	Investment	368.0	370.3	359.8
	GNP	2,469.3	2,473.7	2,413.3
Composition of real GNP (percentage)				
1990	Consumption	65.0	64.9	64.8
	Investment	14.9	14.9	14.9
	GNP	100.0	100.0	100.0
2000	Consumption	65.0	65.0	64.6
	Investment	14.9	15.0	14.9
	GNP	100.0	100.0	100.0

there is a corresponding reduction in the available stock. Over time, the slower growth of capital stock slows the growth of the productive potential of the economy and so reduces the prospective rate of return to capital. In the earlier years, the expenditure reductions are concentrated on consumption rather than investment, since the price impacts of the synfuels policy primarily affect consumption, and because there is a partially offsetting boost to investment due to the capital requirements of these technologies. Later, however, the situation is altered. The proportionate decline in investment accelerates under the dynamic influences of the saving and rate-of-return effects. The consequent slowing of capital growth accentuates the reductions in real GNP due to the efficiency effects.

The burden of economic losses falls relatively more heavily on consumption for the conservation case as well. Under the conservation policy in 1990, consumption absorbs 95 percent of the decline in real GNP, with investment accounting for the remainder. However, in the 1990s, the economy realizes efficiency gains from this policy, so economic growth over the final decade of the century is slightly higher than in the reference case. Investment necessarily grows in a manner consistent with the expansion in real GNP.

The synfuels policy clearly imposes an economic cost in terms of income and production foregone. Not so obvious, however, is whether the conservation policy shows overall net economic costs or benefits in comparison to the reference projection. Therefore, it is useful to develop a measure that represents the policy costs or benefits throughout the entire period 1980 to 2000.

For any two policy cases, a common measure for such representations is provided by the present value of the differences between indicators of economic performance. Computationally, this value accumulates annual differences in economic variables where these are discounted to a near-term reference period through weights that reflect a social rate of time preference. At a zero social rate of discount, the present value simply measures the total cumulative differences. For positive discount rates, the differences occurring in earlier periods are weighted more heavily than those in later ones. Thus, at selected discount rates, the present value formulation permits the determination of overall net policy benefits or costs.

Applying present value formulation to differences in real GNP yields the results shown in Table 6−7. These figures support the conclusion that the policies underlying the reference and conservation cases are more beneficial economically than those for the synfuels projection. However, at reasonable social rates of discount, the conservation policy also involves an economic cost, compared to the reference projection. Only at extremely low discount rates does the conservation policy produce net economic benefits.

The national income accounts give another basis for measuring economic performance. The present value of real personal consump-

Table 6−7. Discounted net benefits of alternative energy policies: GNP effects[a] (*billions of 1972 dollars*).

	Social Discount Rate		
Cases	*0 percent*	*5 percent*	*10 percent*
Reference versus conservation	0.4	−3.7	−4.3
Reference versus synfuels	−410.0	−200.7	−106.7
Synfuels versus conservation	410.4	197.0	102.4

a. Determined as changes between cases in the present value of real GNP.

tion and government purchases, or real private and public consumption is, perhaps, a better indicator of economic welfare than discounted real GNP. Real personal consumption is a direct use of output for the satisfaction of individual preferences. Government purchases are a similar use of output, except that preferences are revealed through the political process and are satisfied collectively.

Figures for differences in discounted consumption and government purchases are shown in Table 6−8. The results here are more decisive; neither of the more active policies is costless when compared to the reference projection. The conservation policy again is preferred to the synfuels program, but the policies of the reference projection are preferable to both.

The policies also differ in their impact on the sectoral patterns of final spending and, hence, the output mix of the economy. Table 6−9 summarizes the sectoral composition of aggregate demand expenditures for the policy alternatives. The most noticeable feature of these results is the energy share of final spending. Conservation both promotes and permits traditional energy expenditures to be redirected toward spending on nonenergy goods and services. These are concentrated, for the most part, on additional purchases from the manufacturing and the trade and services sectors. Thus, relative to the structures of final demand for the other projections, the share of energy is the smallest and the shares of manufacturing and of trade and services are the largest under the conservation policy. The synfuels policy, however, substitutes energy from high-cost technologies for that available from lower cost, conventional sources. Thus, the absolute and relative importance of energy in final demand spending is larger for this projection. The imposition of more expensive energy

Table 6−8. Discounted net benefits of alternative energy policies: consumption effects[a] (*billions of 1972 dollars*).

	Social Discount Rate		
Cases	*0 percent*	*5 percent*	*10 percent*
Reference versus conservation	−10.3	−8.2	−6.2
Reference versus synfuels	−353.7	−173.6	−92.5
Synfuels versus conservation	343.4	165.4	86.3

a. Determined as changes between cases in the present value of real consumption plus government expenditures.

Table 6-9.   Aggregate final demand expenditures.

		Reference	Conservation	Synfuels
Purchases *(billions of 1972 dollars)*				
1990	Agriculture, nonfuel mining, construction	173.0	172.5	171.6
	Manufacturing	522.0	522.4	517.0
	Transportation	66.1	66.0	65.0
	Services	1,157.2	1,167.0	1,146.8
	Energy	77.8	59.6	83.0
2000	Agriculture, nonfuel mining, construction	213.6	212.6	208.8
	Manufacturing	704.1	706.4	687.8
	Transportation	102.1	99.6	99.6
	Services	1,540.7	1,559.0	1,509.7
	Energy	81.9	63.0	83.0
Composition of purchases *(percentage)*				
1990	Agriculture, nonfuel mining, construction	8.67	8.68	8.65
	Manufacturing	26.15	26.28	26.07
	Transportation	3.31	3.32	3.28
	Services	57.97	58.72	57.82
	Energy	3.90	3.00	4.18
2000	Agriculture, nonfuel mining, construction	8.08	8.05	8.07
	Manufacturing	26.65	26.75	26.57
	Transportation	3.86	3.77	3.85
	Services	58.31	59.04	58.31
	Energy	3.10	2.39	3.21

requires a redirection of expenditures on nonenergy goods and services toward energy purchases.

The mix of inputs into production provides the final basis for comparing the three cases. The input–output coefficients for capital, labor, energy, and intermediate materials are presented and compared in Table 6–10. In all cases, the general trend is for the economy to grow continually more capital-intensive and less intensive in the use of labor and energy. However, the magnitude of the changes differs significantly, depending on the policy being considered. By the end of the century, the conservation case is the least labor-intensive, whereas the synfuels policy leads to the greatest labor intensity of aggregate output. Furthermore, the rate of increase in the amount of capital per worker is largest in the conservation case, followed next by the reference projection. Since this is an important factor contributing to the advance of gross labor productivity, it follows that the conservation policy is most beneficial in this respect. The opposite holds for the synfuels policy. Finally, the rate of improvement in the energy efficiency of capital, as measured by the capital–energy ratio, is highest for the conservation case and smallest for the synfuels policy.

The reciprocals of the input–output coefficients—that is, total output per unit of input—also measure productivity. Over the entire projection horizon, the productivities of labor and energy rise the most in the conservation case and the least in the synfuels case. Also, the conservation policy causes the slowest rate of decline in capital productivity, whereas the synfuels policy imposes the largest decrease. These differences in factor productivities contribute mate-

Table 6–10.   Input–Output coefficients for aggregate output.

Year	Factor	Reference Case	Conservation Case	Synfuels Case
1990	Capital	0.1789	0.1794	0.1793
	Labor	0.2077	0.2072	0.2080
	Energy	0.0289	0.0272	0.0298
	Materials	0.5844	0.5862	0.5829
2000	Capital	0.2044	0.2041	0.2052
	Labor	0.1829	0.1815	0.1845
	Energy	0.0279	0.0267	0.0283
	Materials	0.5848	0.5876	0.5819

rially to the macroeconomic impacts that result from the introduction of these policies.

The influences of the policies on the input structure of the economy result from several considerations. First, the policies require a withdrawal of productive resources from other activities within the economy. Simultaneously, they promote the substitution of new energy production techniques, so resources originally dedicated to producing conventional supplies are released. As indicated, the net withdrawals under the synfuels policy are substantially larger than those associated with the conservation policy. Finally, the new levels and structures of final spending under the policies are consistent only with reconfigured input patterns. With equilibrium a requirement in each factor market, these changes influence the relative price structure and so further affect input decisions. The interactions reciprocate as well, insofar as the pattern of input choices has an impact on macroeconomic performance.

For the alternative energy policies, the principal comparative conclusions regarding the growth and structure of the U.S. economy are summarized as follows:

1. The policies have a significant effect on the output and input structures of the economy, with energy changes being both the motivating force and the dominant impact.
2. Positive economic growth at steadily declining rates continues under either the synfuels or the conservation policies.
3. When compared to the reference projection, both policies are seen to impose an economic cost in terms of income and production foregone. However, conservation's impact on macroeconomic performance is neither large nor permanent and is significantly less than that imposed by the synfuels policy.
4. Over the long run, the conservation policy has a favorable effect on productivity, whereas the reverse is true for the synfuels policy.

IV. SENSITIVITY ANALYSES

The measured economic effects of the synfuels and conservation policies are conditional on the specific policy representations introduced into the reference projection. Thus, it is important to examine the sensitivity of these impacts to variations in the policy representations. The macroeconomic results in the subsequent assessments are determined from the application of only the DJA economic model to alternative policy specifications. The results are indicative only of the direction of change rather than the absolute magnitude of change, since the BNL component of the integrated model system was not employed. The information determined in this manner is sufficient for approximating the sensitivity of the economic effects to policy variations.

The economic effects of conservation depend on the timing of conservation expenditures, the pattern of energy savings by fuel type, and the effectiveness of conservation policy.

The first of these refers to the annualization schemes applied to the cost information from the CSE program documentation. Given the nature of discounting, a particular level of discounted cost can be associated with an infinite number of annual expenditure patterns and, hence, cumulative undiscounted cost levels. Changes in the time pattern and levels of annual conservation expenditures affect whether the policy imposes a net economic cost or leads to a net economic benefit. These variations also affect the time horizons over which net costs are incurred or net benefits are realized; that is, the timing of benefits and costs as measured by increases and decreases from the reference case–levels of real GNP.

For each subprogram, one of three distributional rules or patterns was selected to annualize the total expenditure data: the uniform, the constant-rate-of-growth, and the trapezoidal. Of these, only the latter two are important to the sensitivity analyses. The programs to which the uniform distribution was applied have virtually no private-sector content, so a reliable time pattern of expenditure is provided in the CSE program materials.

Several parameters for the remaining two distributional rules can be varied to affect the time pattern and annual level of conservation outlays. For the constant-rate-of-growth subprograms, these include program duration and the annual rate of expenditure growth over this interval. For the trapezoidal distributions, variations can be made in the lengths of the growth, uniform, and decline intervals, and the rates of expenditure growth and decline occurring in the first and last of these periods. Changes in the overall annual cost of conservation, and, hence, its economic impact, were analyzed by systematically and sequentially varying these annualization parameters,

Table 6–11. Effects on total annual policy costs and economic performance of combined variations in the annualization schemes for conservation subprograms.

Policy Variation	Total Resource Claims Due to Conservation Policy (Billions of 1972 Dollars)		GNP (Billions of 1972 Dollars)	
	1990	2000	1990	2000
Reference projection	—	—	1,901.3	2,469.3
Original conservation specification	14.2	24.2	1,899.1	2,473.7
I	10.1	37.1	1,904.0	2,456.3
II	18.6	40.5	1,893.9	2,447.5
III	15.4	47.2	1,898.0	2,438.0
IV	12.1	13.1	1,901.3	2,491.6
V	20.7	16.5	1,891.4	2,482.9
VI	17.4	23.2	1,895.4	2,473.6

then simulating the performance of the economy under the new conservation cost conditions.

These detailed assessments established the sensitivity of the total annual costs of conservation policy to sequential changes in the annual expenditure patterns. In addition, indications were given as to the directional influence of these isolated changes on economic performance. As the logical final step of this analysis, it is important to combine alternative policy cases and to examine more explicitly the economic effects associated with these reconfigurations. The objective in collectively varying these parameters is to identify a plausible range of economic effects conditional on one of the more important classes of analytical assumptions. Thus, the parametric changes underlying the detailed sensitivity analyses were grouped in accordance with this objective. Table 6–11 shows the effects on real GNP and the total resource claims of conservation from selected alternative policy representations. It can be seen that, with no modifications to either the total discounted policy costs or the energy savings, there are wide variations in the pattern of economic growth. Equally significant are the cumulative economic effects of temporal variations in the expenditure levels and patterns. The discounted net benefits of conservation policy are presented in Table 6–12. From

Table 6–12.   Discounted net benefits of conservation policy[a] (*billions of 1972 dollars*).

Policy Variation	Social Discount Rate		
	0 percent	5 percent	10 percent
Original conservation specification	0.4	−3.7	−4.3
I	−39.3	−12.4	−2.5
II	−185.2	−93.8	−51.7
III	−192.8	−89.9	−45.2
IV	113.5	49.5	22.7
V	−30.1	−30.6	−25.6
VI	−37.2	−26.6	−19.1

a. Determined as changes in the present value of real GNP measured from the reference projection.

this, the policy can be seen to impose a macroeconomic cost as large as $193 billion (1972) or lead to an overall net economic benefit of $114 billion (1972). However, even the case least advantageous to conservation is significantly less damaging to the economy compared to the $410 billion (1972) cumulative net cost determined for the synfuels policy.

The second major area of sensitivity for the conservation policy concerns the division of energy savings among petroleum, natural gas, and electricity. Variations in the pattern of these savings can affect significantly the timing and magnitude of net benefits or costs. In terms of their real input claims on the economy, electricity, petroleum, and natural gas are the most, second most, and least expensive, respectively. Consequently, the more electricity that is displaced through conservation, the larger (smaller) are the net economic benefits (costs) from conservation policy. To illustrate this point, three alternatives to the original conservation projection are specified. The total amount of primary energy savings is the same for all cases. Further, the displacement of petroleum, and, hence, the value of this displacement, is the same for the three alternatives. The differences among them center on the allocation of nonpetroleum savings to crude natural-gas and electricity inputs. These differences lead to differences in the total quantity and mix of the delivered energy that is conserved. More important, the configurations are different with respect to the total value and input composition of the resources released from energy production. In the first of these cases, the non-petroleum energy savings are biased toward the conservation of inputs to electricity. In the second case, the nonpetroleum primary energy savings are divided equally between natural gas and electricity. In the third alternative, the gas–electricity split of the first case is reversed, so most of the conservation is allocated to the savings of utility gas. The macroeconomic impacts and net policy benefits for these alternatives are shown in Table 6–13. The policy implication of these results is clear. In designing conservation policies that jointly promote national energy, economic, and environmental objectives, the net economic benefits are greatest (or, the costs are least) for strategies that place relative emphasis on substitutions away from petroleum *and* electricity.

Finally, for conservation, there is the issue of policy effectiveness. The controllable instrument for this policy is represented by the government outlays associated with each conservation subprogram. The desired effect of the government programs is to motivate the private sector to redirect its purchases toward conservation activities. This ultimately provides the energy savings, which are the basis for the direct and indirect economic benefits (or costs) from conservation policy. However, the levels of private expenditure and the resultant energy savings that are realized from the government incentives are the outputs of the policy. As such, they are, to some extent, uncontrollable. For the given levels of public and private expenditure, the energy savings could be significantly less than anticipated; conversely, the anticipated energy savings might be attained only at a substantially higher cost. To examine the economic consequences of these, two cases are considered. In the first, the energy savings achieved for the given levels of total expenditure were taken to be half of those obtained in the original assessment. The mix of these savings, however, was unaffected. For the second case, the original levels and mix of energy savings were presumed to be attained at double the original cost. Both these cases have the effect of increasing by twofold the unit cost of energy from conservation. However, their economic impacts will differ, as each case implies a different structural mix and level of resource claims and releases due to conservation policy. The effects on real GNP and the discounted net benefits of these variations are presented in Table 6–14. Doubling the policy cost has approximately twice the impact of the halving of

Table 6–13. Impacts on economic performance and benefits of varying the mix of energy savings from conservation.

Policy Variation	GNP (Billions of 1972 Dollars)		Discounted Net Benefits at Selected Social Discount Rates[a] (Billions of 1972 Dollars)		
	1990	2000	0 percent	5 percent	10 percent
Reference projection	1,901.3	2,469.3	—	—	—
Original conservation projection	1,899.1	2,473.7	0.4	–3.7	–4.3
Electricity bias[b]	1,902.1	2,486.5	95.6	43.1	20.7
Equal division[b]	1,900.0	2,478.4	33.3	12.2	4.1
Natural-gas bias[b]	1,898.1	2,470.2	–27.5	–17.6	–11.8

a. Determined as changes in the present value of real GNP measured from the reference projection.
b. Refers to division of primary, nonpetroleum energy savings between inputs to electricity and crude natural gas.

Table 6-14. Impacts on economic performance and benefits of varying the effectiveness of the conservation policy.

Policy Variation	GNP (Billions of 1972 Dollars)		Discounted Net Benefits at Selected Social Discount Rates[a] (Billions of 1972 Dollars)		
	1990	2000	0 percent	5 percent	10 percent
Reference projection	1,901.3	2,469.3	—	—	—
Original conservation projection	1,899.1	2,473.7	0.4	-3.7	-4.3
Double policy costs	1,881.9	2,431.4	-387.5	-203.3	-116.0
Halve energy savings	1,891.2	2,450.6	-196.4	-103.5	-59.3

a. Determined as changes in the present value of real GNP measured from the reference projection.

the energy savings. As indicated, this difference is attributable to the level and compositional implications of these changes. More important, however, is the comparison of the effects of these variations to the results for the synfuels policy. For the net economic costs of the two policies to be equal requires either a doubling of the unit cost of energy from conservation or the virtual elimination of energy savings from the given levels of effort.

However, the issue of effectiveness also extends to the synfuels policy. In developing the synfuels projection, the input requirements for each technology were time-invariant. No consideration was given to cost reductions due to learning effects, technical improvements, economies of scale, or other types of productivity advance. Changes in the costs of fuels from the synthetic and unconventional sources can affect significantly the net economic cost associated with this policy. Three variations are considered: a doubling of the synfuels costs, a halving of these costs, and the situation in which synfuels are competitive with the energy made available from conservation. Table 6-15 presents the impacts on economic performance and net policy benefits resulting from these changes. These results clearly demonstrate the benefit potential of directing the synfuel programs toward the promotion of accelerated cost reduction rather than accelerated commercial deployment. Reducing the costs of these fuels to the point at which they are competitive with the energy made available from conservation more than halves the adverse macroeconomic impact of the synfuels policy.

That there still is a significant economic cost, as compared to conservation, results from two considerations. First, the mix of energy displacements and its valuation are substantially different between the two policies. The synfuels policy is not directed toward the displacement of energy in general or of electricity in particular. Rather, it focuses on the production of petroleum and gas products by means other than importation. The effect of this focus can be inferred from the analysis of the pattern of energy savings, by fuel type, from conservation. As little electricity is displaced, the synfuels policy imposes a net cost on the economy that is directionally the same as was observed for conservation with a natural-gas bias (Table 6-13). Second, and more important, there are large differences in the composition of the resource claims—that is, policy costs—between the two policies. For the same unit cost of energy, the synfuels policy is relatively more capital- and less labor-intensive than the conservation

Table 6–15. Impacts on economic performance and benefits of varying the effectiveness of the synfuels policy.

Policy Variation	GNP (Billions of 1972 Dollars)		Discounted Net Benefits at Selected Social Discount Rates [a] (Billions of 1972 Dollars)		
	1990	2000	0 percent	5 percent	10 percent
Reference projection	1,901.3	2,469.3	—	—	—
Original synfuels projection	1,888.9	2,413.3	−410.0	−200.7	−106.7
Double technology costs	1,880.7	2,373.1	−698.0	−340.8	−180.7
Halve technology costs	1,895.0	2,433.4	−246.2	−118.5	−61.8
Synfuels costs competitive with energy made available from conservation	1,896.9	2,441.4	−186.4	−89.0	−46.0

a. Determined as changes in the present value of real GNP measured from the reference projection.

policy. The process of capital formation is crucial to economic growth, and thus, factors that affect it relatively more have a relatively larger impact on economic performance. Since the synfuels policy involves a relatively larger diversion of capital service inputs from other productive uses, its economic consequence is larger than that for conservation, even though the unit costs of energy are the same.

V. POLICY IMPLICATIONS

The results from this analysis yield important implications for the focus and direction of U.S. energy policy. Each strategy succeeds in reducing the nation's import dependence. In the reference projection, the influences of import quotas and domestic oil and gas price decontrol result in a halving of oil imports relative to the current levels of approximately 8 million barrels per day. These influences also serve to slow the annual rate of growth of primary energy consumption to well under 2 percent and promote a shift in energy-use patterns toward a greater utilization of coal. The introduction of the conservation or the synfuels policy further reduces U.S. import requirements, with the conservation policy being slightly more effective. Under the conservation policy, oil imports are reduced from the reference case levels by 3.5 and 8.4 quadrillion Btu for the years 1990 and 2000, respectively. The corresponding reductions for the synfuels policy are 3.2 and 7.0 quadrillion Btu. Either of these policies permits the almost total elimination of imports by the year 2000. From conservation, there is the additional benefit that the growth in aggregate primary energy demand is virtually halted. For the years 1990 and 2000, total primary energy savings from conservation are 10.3 and 22.3 quadrillion Btu, respectively. However, even the large-scale introduction of synthetic fuels results in only marginally higher primary energy consumption than in the reference case, being only 2.0 and 2.9 quadrillion Btu higher in the respective years. Thus, to different degrees, energy conservation is evident under all three of the strategies.

It is in the environmental and economic areas that the strategies differ the most.[4] For the environment, an ordering of the strategies indicates that substantial environmental benefits are obtainable from energy conservation. In addition to the emissions reductions associated with the decreased use of petroleum and natural gas, there are significant improvements in environmental quality attributable to the slower growth of total coal consumption and nuclear inputs into electric generation. Relative to the reference projection, future nuclear power requirements are decreased by 30 to 40 percent due to the successes of the conservation programs. Also, by 2000, conservation has led to a 9.1 quadrillion Btu reduction in annual coal use, down almost 20 percent from the reference case amount. The energy reductions from conservation provide important benefits in the forms of less damage to land, improvements in air and water quality, and increased public health and safety. However, these benefits are increasingly lost in moving to the policies that characterize the reference and synfuels projections.

For the economy, the introduction of the synfuels policy imposes significant net economic cost. Real GNP is projected to be $1,888.9 billion and $2,413.3 billion (1972) for 1990 and 2000, respectively. The growth in real GNP is lower for this case than for either the reference or the conservation projections. Relative to the former, the synfuels policy results in a cumulative macroeconomic cost between $410.0 billion and $106.7 billion (1972), depending on the choice of discount rate.

The conservation results are mixed. Relative to the reference projection, the conservation policy leads to lower and higher levels of economic activity in 1990 and 2000, respectively. The differences are small, $2.2 billion (1972) in 1990 and $4.4 billion (1972) in 2000. When discounting these annual real GNP differences, the conservation policy provides cumulative net economic benefits only at extremely low social rates of discount. At more reasonable discount rates, such as 5 or 10 percent, conservation results in a cumulative net economic cost of less than $5.0 billion (1972).

The conclusions derived for the policy cases are sensitive to, inter alia, the actual policy representations introduced into the analysis. The evidence of Section IV suggests that there are reasonable circumstances under which the conservation and synfuels policies become less and more favorable, respectively. In these cases and in terms of macroeconomic effects, the decisive comparative advantage of conservation over supply expansion begins to erode. However, for the supply policy to be judged economically superior to the conservation strategy, relatively extreme combinations of policy assumptions biased against demand reduction and for accelerated synthetic and unconventional fuels development are required.

From the above comparisons, it seems clear that conservation, even in isolation from other policies, can play a major role in alleviating the import dependence problem and slowing the growth of energy demand. These are achieved at only a small macroeconomic cost and with substantial environmental benefits. Further, conservation compares favorably to the synfuels policy. It is slightly more successful in reducing imports and provides the best mechanism for reducing demand growth. Relative to the reference projection, there are environmental costs from the synfuels policy, whereas, with conservation, there are significant improvements in environmental quality. Finally, the relative impacts on economic performance are much less severe from conservation policy than from the synfuels program.

These conclusions do not deny a benefit potential from current synfuels policies. Nor should they be interpreted as advocating a de-escalation of supply expansion programs. The favorable economic results for conservation policy as compared to synfuels are directly attributable to the policy costs of each program. In terms of only the program costs, the conservation policy provides energy at a lower cost than that of the fuels it displaces. The converse is true for the synfuels policy. For example, the 1990 cost of energy from conservation is $2.10 (1978) per million Btu, while the cost of energy from synfuels is $5.25 (1978) per million Btu. This suggests that synfuels programs directed toward cost reduction and the resolution of environmental issues are more appropriate than those that promote the accelerated commercial deployment of current technologies.

NOTES TO CHAPTER 6

1. For a complete presentation of the analysis and its conclusions, see Davitian et al. (1979).
2. For the text of the President's speech, see Associated Press and the *Boston Globe* (1979).
3. See the text of the President's speech, as found in Associated Press and the *Boston Globe* (1979). See also *Coal R and D* (1979).
4. See the complete representation of the results of this analysis in Davitian et al. (1979).

BIBLIOGRAPHY

Adelman, M. 1972. *The World Petroleum Market*. Baltimore: Johns Hopkins University Press.

Alterman, J. 1977. "The Energy/Real Gross Domestic Product Ratio—An Analysis of Changes During the 1966–1970 Period in Relation to Long-Run Trends." Staff Paper no. 30, Bureau of Economic Analysis, U.S. Department of Commerce. Washington, D.C.

Associated Press and the *Boston Globe*. 1979 (July 16). Text of President Carter's speech to the nation.

Berndt, E.R. 1976. "Reconciling Alternative Estimates of the Elasticity of Substitution." *The Review of Economics and Statistics* 58, no. 1 (February): 59–67.

Berndt, E.R., and D.O. Wood. 1975. "Technology, Prices, and the Derived Demand for Energy." *The Review of Economics and Statistics* 57, no. 3 (August): 259–68.

_____. 1979. "Engineering and Econometric Interpretations of Energy–Capital Complementarity." *American Economic Review* 69, no. 3 (June): 342–54.

Berner, R. 1976. "A General Equilibrium Model of International Discrimination." Ph.D. dissertation, University of Pennsylvania.

Berner, R.; P. Clark; J. Enzler; and B. Lowrey. 1975. "International Sources of Domestic Inflation." *Studies in Price Stability and Economic Growth*. Joint Economic Committee (August 5). Washington, D.C.: Government Printing Office.

Berner, R.; P. Clark; E. Hernandez-Cata; H. Howe; S. Kwack; and G. Stevens. Forthcoming. *A Multi-country Model of the International Influences on the U.S. Economy*.

157

Branson, W., and J. Rotemberg. 1979. "International Adjustment with Wage Rigidity." Working Paper no. 406, National Bureau of Economic Research. Cambridge, Mass.

Braun, A. 1976. "Indexation of Wages and Salaries in the Developed Countries." *International Monetary Fund Staff Papers* 23: 226-71.

Bruno, M., and J. Sachs. In press. "Supply Versus Demand Approaches to the Problem of Stagflation." *Weltwirtschaftliches Archiv.*

Bullard, C. 1978. "Discussion." *American Economic Review* 68, no. 2, p. 125.

Cagan, P. 1980. "Imported Inflation 1973-74 and the Accommodation Issue." *Journal of Money, Credit and Banking* 12: 1-16.

Coal R and D. 1979. Vol. 2, no. 84 (August 1).

Darmstadter, J. and H. Landsberg. 1975. "The Economic Background." *Daedalus* 104, no. 4 (Fall): 15-37.

Darmstadter, J., J. Dunkerley, and J. Alterman. 1977. *How Industrial Societies Use Energy.* Baltimore: Johns Hopkins University Press.

Davitian, H.; P.J. Groncki; P. Kleeman; J. Lukachinski; R.J. Goettle; and E.A. Hudson. 1979 (October). *A Strategic Cost-Benefit Analysis of Energy Policies: Overview*, BNL 51105; *Detailed Projections*, BNL 51127; *Comparative Analysis*, BNL 51128. Upton, N.Y.: Brookhaven National Laboratory.

Denison, E. 1979. "Explanations of Declining Productivity Growth. *Survey of Current Business* 59, no. 8, pt. 2 (August): 1-24.

Dohner, R. 1978. "Terms of Trade Changes and the Domestic Inflationary Process." Unpublished paper, Massachusetts Institute of Technology.

Dornbusch, R., and S. Fischer. 1978. *Macroeconomics.* New York: McGraw-Hill.

Eckstein, O. 1978. *The Great Recession, with a Postscript on Stagflation.* Data Resources Series, vol. 3. New York: North-Holland Publishing Company.

Fair, R. 1978 (June). "Inflation and Unemployment in a Macroeconomic Model." In *After the Phillips Curve: Persistence of High Inflation and High Unemployment.* Conference Series, no. 19, Federal Reserve Bank of Boston.

Fried, E., and C. Schultze, eds. 1975. *Higher Oil Prices and the World Economy.* Washington, D.C.: Brookings Institution.

Godley, W., and W.D. Nordhaus. 1972. "Pricing in the Trade Cycle." *Economic Journal* 82: 853-82.

Goldfeld, S.M. 1973. "The Demand for Money Revisited." *Brookings Papers on Economic Activity* 3: 577-646.

_____. 1976. "The Case of the Missing Money." *Brookings Papers on Economic Activity* 3: 683-730.

Gordon, R.J. 1975a. "Alternative Responses of Policy to External Supply Shocks." *Brookings Papers on Economic Activity* 1: 183-206.

_____. 1975b. "The Impact of Aggregate Demand on Prices." *Brookings Papers on Economic Activity* 3: 613-62.

_____. 1977. "Can The Inflation of the 1970s Be Explained?" *Brookings Papers on Economic Activity* 1: 253-79.

Gramlich, E. 1979. "Macro Policy Responses to Price Shocks." *Brookings Papers on Economic Activity* 1: 128–33.

Griffin, J.M., and P.A. Gregory. 1976. "Intercountry Translog Model of Energy Substitution Responses." *American Economic Review* 66, no. 5 (December): 845–57.

Hall, R.E. 1977. "Investment, Interest Rates, and the Effects of Stabilization Policies." *Brookings Papers on Economic Activity* 1: 61–121.

_____. 1978a. "The Macroeconomic Impact of Changes in Income Taxes in the Short and Medium Runs." *Journal of Political Economy* 86, no. 2, pt. 2 (April): S71–S85.

_____. 1978b. "Stochastic Implications of the Life Cycle–Permanent Income Hypothesis: Theory and Evidence." *Journal of Political Economy* 86, no. 6 (December): 971–87.

Hausman, J. 1979. "Consumer Choice of Durables and Energy Demand." *Bell Journal of Economics* 10, no. 1 (Spring): 33–54.

Hirst, E., and J. Carney. 1979. "The ORNL Residential Energy Use Model." *Land Economics* 55, no. 3: 319–33.

Hogan, W. 1979. "Capital–Energy Complementarity in Aggregate Energy–Economic Analysis," E–79–03. Discussion Paper Series, Kennedy School of Government, Harvard University. Cambridge, Mass.

Hogan, W., and A. Manne. 1977. "Energy–Economy Interactions: The Fable of the Elephant and the Rabbit." In *Modeling Energy–Economy Interactions: Five Approaches*. edited by C. Hitch. Research Paper R–5. Resources for the Future. Washington, D.C.

Hooper, P., and B. Lowrey. 1979 (January). "Impact of the Dollar Depreciation on the U.S. Price Level: An Analytical Survey of Empirical Estimates." International Finance Discussion Paper no. 128, International Finance Division, Board of Governors of the Federal Reserve System. Washington, D.C.

Hudson, E.A., and D.W. Jorgenson. 1977 (September). *The Long-term Interindustry Transactions Model for Energy and Economic Analysis*. Final Report to the Applied Economics Division, Federal Preparedness Agency, General Services Administration. Washington, D.C.

_____. 1978a. "Energy Policy and U.S. Economic Growth." *American Economic Review* 68, no. 2 (May): 118–22.

_____. 1978b. "Energy Prices and the U.S. Economy, 1972–1976." *Natural Resources Journal* 18, no. 4 (October): 877–97.

Klein, L.R. 1978 (June). "Disturbances to the International Economy." *After the Phillips Curve: Persistence of High Inflation and High Unemployment*. Conference Series, no. 19, Federal Reserve Bank of Boston.

Kydes, A.S., and J. Rabinowitz. 1979 (August). *The Time-stepped Energy System Optimization Model (TESOM): Overview and Special Features*. Upton, N.Y.: Brookhaven National Laboratory.

Laursen, S., and L. Metzler. 1950. "Flexible Exchange Rates and the Theory of Employment." *Review of Economics and Statistics* 32, no. 4: 281–99.

Lenczowski, G. 1975. "The Oil Producing Countries." *Daedalus* 104, no. 4 (Fall): 59–72.

LeRoy, D. 1978. "Scheduled Wage Increases and Escalator Provisions in 1978." *Monthly Labor Review* 101, no. 1 (1978): 3–8.

Lukachinski, J.; P.J. Groncki; R.G. Tessmer; R.J. Goettle; and E.A. Hudson. 1979 (October). *An Integrated Methodology for Assessing Energy-Economy Interactions*, BNL 26452. Upton, N.Y.: Brookhaven National Laboratory.

Mancke, R. 1975. *Performance of the Federal Energy Office*. National Energy Study no. 6, American Enterprise Institute. Washington, D.C.

_____ . 1980. "The American Response: On the Job Training?" *Orbis* 23, no. 4: 785–802.

McNees, S. 1976. "The Forecasting Performance in the Early 1970s." *New England Economic Review*, July/August, pp. 29–40.

_____ . 1979. "The Forecasting Record for the 1970s." *New England Economic Review*, September/October, pp. 33–53.

Miller, M. 1976. "Can a Rise in Import Prices Be Inflationary and Deflationary?" *American Economic Review* 66, no. 4 (September): 501–14.

Mishkin, F. 1977. "What Depressed the Consumer? The Household Balance Sheet in the 1973–75 Recession." *Brookings Papers on Economic Activity* 1: 123–64.

Mork, K.A. 1978a. "Aggregate Technology, Biased Productivity Growth, and the Demand for Primary Energy in the U.S. 1949–75." In *1978 Proceedings of the Business and Economics Section of the American Statistical Association*, pp. 482–86. Washington, D.C.: ASA.

_____ . 1978b (June). "Why Are Prices So Rigid?" MIT Energy Laboratory Working Paper no. MIT–EL 78–009WP, MIT Energy Laboratory. Cambridge, Mass.

_____ . 1980 (May). "Energy Prices, Substitution Elasticities, and Economic Growth." Draft paper, MIT Energy Laboratory. Cambridge, Mass.

Mork, K.A., and R.E. Hall. 1980a. "Energy Prices and the U.S. Economy in 1979–1981." *The Energy Journal* 1, no. 2 (April): 41–53.

_____ . 1980b. "Energy Prices, Inflation, and Recession, 1974–1975." *The Energy Journal* 1, no. 3 (July): 31–63.

Nordhaus, W.D. 1972. "Recent Developments in Price Dynamics." In *The Econometrics of Price Determination*, edited by O. Eckstein. Washington, D.C.: Federal Reserve Board.

Office of the White House Press Secretary. 1979. "The White House Fact Sheet on the President's Program." Memo, 9:00 P.M. EST, April 5.

Organization of Economic Cooperation and Development. 1977. *Towards Full Employment and Price Stability*. A report to the OECD by a group of independent experts (McCracken report), Paris: OECD.

Penrose, E. 1975. "The Development of Crisis." *Daedalus* 104, no. 4 (Fall): 39–57.

Perry, G.L. 1975a. "Policy Alternatives for 1974." *Brookings Papers on Economic Activity* 1: 222–35.

_____. 1975b. "The United States." In *Higher Oil Prices and the World Economy*, edited by E. Fried and C. Schultze. Washington, D.C.: The Brookings Institution.

_____. 1978. "Potential Output: Recent Issues and Past Trends." *U.S. Productive Capacity: Estimating the Utilization Gap*. Working Paper no. 23, Center for the Study of American Business. St. Louis, Mo.

Phelps, C., and R. Smith. 1977. "Petroleum Regulation: The False Dilemma of Decontrol." Report no. 2–1951–RC. The Rand Corporation. Santa Monica, Calif.

Phelps, E. 1978. "Commodity Supply Shocks and Full Employment Monetary Policy." *Journal of Money, Credit, and Banking* 10, no. 2: 206–21.

Pierce, J.L., and J.J. Enzler. 1974. "The Effects of External Inflationary Shocks." *Brookings Papers on Economic Activity* 1: 13–61.

Rasche, R., and J. Tatom. 1977a (May). "The Effects of the New Energy Regime on Economic Capacity, Production, and Prices." *Federal Reserve Bank of St. Louis Review*, pp. 2–12.

_____. 1977b (June). "Energy Resources and Potential GNP." *Federal Reserve Bank of St. Louis Review*, pp. 10–24.

Sachs, J. 1979. "Wages, Profits, and Macroeconomic Adjustment in the 1970s: A Comparative Study." *Brookings Papers on Economic Activity* 2: 269–319.

Salant, W.S. 1977. "International Transmission of Inflation." In *Worldwide Inflation: Theory and Recent Experience*, edited by L.B. Krause and W.S. Salant. Washington, D.C.: The Brookings Institution.

_____. 1978. "Trade Balances in Current and Constant Prices When the Terms of Trade Change." In *Breadth and Depth in Economics*, edited by J. Dreyer. Lexington, Mass.: Heath.

Solow, J. 1979. "A General Equilibrium Approach to Aggregate Capital–Energy Complementarity." *Economic Letters* 2: 91–94.

Solow, R. 1980. "What to Do (Macroeconomically) When OPEC Comes." In *Rational Expectations and Economic Policy*, edited by S. Fischer. Chicago: University of Chicago Press (for the National Bureau of Economic Research).

Stobaugh, R. 1975. "The Oil Companies in the Crisis." *Daedalus* 104, no. 4 (Fall): 180–81.

Thurman, S.S. 1977a (April). "The International Sector." Memo, Board of Governors of the Federal Reserve System. Washington, D.C.

_____. 1977b (April). "The Price Sector." Memo, Board of Governors of the Federal Reserve System. Washington, D.C.

_____. 1979. "International Price Linkages: An Analysis from the Standpoint of a Large Econometric Model of the United States Economy." Ph.D. dissertation, George Washington University.

Thurman, S.S., and S.Y. Kwack. 1976. "Linking the MPS Price Sector to International Price Disturbances." In *Proceedings of the Second Pacific Basin Central Bank Conference on Economic Modeling,* Seoul, Korea, June 8–11, pp. 286–302.

Urdang, E.S. 1979. "An International Flow of Funds Model with an Endogenous Exchange Rate." Ph.D. dissertation, University of Pennsylvania.

U.S. Congress. 1980 (March). Joint Economic Committee. Committee Print, 96th Cong., 8th sess.

U.S. Department of Energy, Conservation and Solar Energy, Office of Policy, Planning, and Evaluation. 1978 (August). *Consolidated Ranking of Fiscal Year 1980 Decision Packages.* Washington, D.C.: U.S. DOE.

U.S. Department of Energy. 1979a (May). *National Energy Plan II.* Washington, D.C.: U.S. DOE.

U.S. Department of Energy, Energy Information Administration. 1979b (July). *Annual Report to Congress: 1978,* DOE/EIA-0173/3. Washington, D.C.: Government Printing Office.

Verleger, P. 1979. "The U.S. Petroleum Crisis of 1979." *Brookings Papers on Economic Activity* 2: 463–75.

Von Furstenberg, G.M., and B.G. Malkiel. 1977. "The Government and Capital Formation: A Survey of Recent Issues." *Journal of Economic Literature* 15, no. 3 (September): 835–78.

Wilkinson, F., and H. Turner. 1972. "The Wage-Tax Spiral and Labor Militancy." In *Do Trade Unions Cause Inflation?,* edited by D. Jackson et al. Cambridge: Cambridge University Press.

INDEX

ABOUT THE CONTRIBUTORS

Robert E. Hall is a well-known macroeconomist. He is Professor of Economics at Stanford University and Senior Fellow at the Hoover Institution at Stanford University. Professor Hall is a member of the Brookings Panel on Economic Activity and has made numerous contributions to its *Papers*. The results of his research on employment and wage inflation and on consumer behavior are widely known and appreciated.

Otto Eckstein is Paul M. Warburg Professor of Economics at Harvard University and President of Data Resources, Inc. He did pioneering research on inflation in the United States and has published numerous books and articles on a broad range of macroeconomic issues. His recent book, *The Great Recession*, and his forthcoming book on core inflation are closely related to his contribution to the present volume.

Robert S. Dohner is Assistant Professor at the Fletcher School of Law and Diplomacy, Tufts University. He received his Ph.D. in economics from M.I.T. His dissertation as well as ensuing papers centered around the impact on wage inflation of changes in the prices for energy and other imported goods.

Stephan Thurman and **Richard Berner** are currently staff economists at Wharton Econometric Forecasting Associates. Their contribution to this volume was made while both served as economists for the Board of Governors of the Federal Reserve System. Dr. Berner has contributed to a congressional study on the international sources of domestic inflation and a forthcoming book on the international influences on the U.S. economy. Dr. Thurman has written several papers on international linkages to the U.S. price system.

Richard J. Goettle IV is currently a senior economist at Dale W. Jorgenson Associates. He has previously done research and energy policy analysis at Brookhaven National Laboratory. He is one of the main contributors to the Dale W. Jorgenson Associates/Brookhaven National Laboratory integrated energy–economic model system.

ABOUT THE EDITOR

Knut Anton Mork is a Research Associate at the M.I.T. Energy Laboratory. His research over the last three years has been devoted to the effects of energy price shocks on inflation, employment, and economic activity. He has authored several articles on the subject. One article, published in *The Energy Journal*, analyzed the role of the OPEC oil price increase in the 1974–1975 experience of simultaneous inflation and recession. Another article applied a similar analysis to the situation after the Iranian revolution in 1979. Both articles were co-authored by Robert E. Hall. Dr. Mork's research on the short-term effects of energy price shocks has emphasized integrated analysis of the supply and demand sides of the economy.

Dr. Mork was born in Norway in 1946. He studied economics at the Norwegian School of Economics and Business Administration in Bergen before coming to the United States in 1974. He received his Ph.D. in Economics from M.I.T. in 1977.